Early Praise for *Par~~is Lost and Found~~*

T0245743

"Lovers of Paris know that Scott Car~~penter~~ authentic city behind the iconic sigh~~ts. In addition~~ to his delightful, insightful *French L~~ike Moi, he adds a~~ deeply personal journey, illuminating~~ the City of~~ Light, and loss, and love."

—Don George, author of The Way of Wanderlust

"Almost all stories set in Paris benefit from the reflected glow of the City of Light. But Carpenter has a unique way of seeing the world around him that elevates even the most mundane encounters of everyday life in the 13th arrondissement with curiosity, tenderness, and humor. He writes with a seemingly effortless lightness that's deceptively hard to achieve in memoir writing, making the reader laugh out loud, even as he shares his journey navigating the sorrow of his own loss. Honestly, the funniest book I've ever read that also made me cry."

—Heather Stimmler, editor of Secrets of Paris

"Not only the best travel book I've read all year, but one of the most satisfying books I've read this decade."

—Gillian Kendall, Perceptive Travel, and author of Mr. Ding's Chicken Feet

"Directed by his Midwestern sense of delight, Carpenter adopts the role of an American observer, making keen observations about language and about the fact that human vulnerability makes people more alike than they are different. Still, everyone Carpenter encounters is fair game for an affectionate portrait that speaks to their particular quirks and culture. A nuanced memoir about loss, starting over, and embracing a new home abroad."

—Foreword Clarion Reviews

"Five Stars" —*Readers' Favorite*

Praise for *French Like Moi*

"Many entertaining anecdotes and worthy observations about French and American culture…Carpenter's droll take keeps the reader chuckling."

—Minneapolis Star Tribune

"Thanks to Scott Carpenter's funny new book…we can experience day-to-day life in a condo that is not in the fancy part of the city. Grab a drink, head to a cool place and meet a delightful cast of Parisians."

—Twin Cities Pioneer Press

"A delightful read...filled with levity and grace. A winning and witty collection offering humor and insight into the French way of life."

—*Kirkus Reviews*

"*French Like Moi* tours the everyday Paris that's found away from Eiffel Tower tourism. With an entertaining guide at the helm, bon mots and corny puns find a home alongside solid timing, curious anecdotes, and self-aware mocking. This quirky travel memoir uncovers lesser-known facets with verve."

—*Foreword Reviews*, Editor's Pick

"In this funny memoir...Carpenter has a knack for turning potential catastrophes into comedy. Readers will find plenty to appreciate in his sharp take on expat life."

—*Publishers Weekly*

"Carpenter shares hilarious faux pas and cultural differences, reading with a deadpan, self-deprecating, understated tone. An affectionate, insider's look at French culture."

—*Booklist*, Audiobook

"Carpenter captures the ironies, oddities, and attractions of the French capital in a way few writers have achieved—which is saying a lot, considering how many have tried their hand at conjuring the City of Light.... *French Like Moi* is a delightful romp through French life and Midwestern sensibilities, all combined in one compelling story."

—*Midwest Book Review*

"Loaded with lacerating wit and trenchant but tender observations, Scott Carpenter's *French Like Moi* is also a true original: a serious memoir that doesn't take itself too seriously. It is this humility that gives Carpenter's book its undeniable strength—that, and his vivid, often hilarious storytelling."

—Marcia DeSanctis, *New York Times* bestselling author of
100 Places in France Every Woman Should Go

"I laughed until my sides hurt at Carpenter's lighthearted and self-deprecating take on living in *l'Hexagone*. For loyal lovers of Paris and France, and anyone who's moved abroad or is thinking about it, *French Like Moi* is a jovial reminder to pack your patience and your dictionary, and gobble up every single, butter-soaked morsel of the journey."

—Kimberley Lovato, author of *Walnut Wine & Truffle Groves*

PARIS
LOST AND
FOUND

PARIS
LOST AND
FOUND

A Memoir of Love

SCOTT DOMINIC CARPENTER

TRAVELERS' TALES
AN IMPRINT OF SOLAS HOUSE, INC.
PALO ALTO

Travelers' Tales and Solas House are trademarks of Solas House, Inc., Palo Alto, California
travelerstales.com | solashouse.com

Art Direction: Kimberly Nelson
Cover Design: Kimberly Nelson
Interior Design and Page Layout: Howie Severson
Map Illustration: Liam Golden
Author Photo: Bonnie Harris

Library of Congress Cataloging-in-Publication Data is available upon request.

978-1-60952-212-4 (paperback)
978-1-60952-213-1 (ebook)
978-1-60952-214-8 (audiobook)

First Edition
Printed in the United States
10 9 8 7 6 5 4 3 2

For Paul & Muriel.
You know why.

Table of Contents

France is a paradise inhabited by people
who believe they're in hell.

—Sylvain Tesson

Rue Bobillot

PART ONE

The End

However, when nothing survives from the distant past,
after the people are dead and the things destroyed, taste
and smell alone—more frail but more enduring, more
intangible, more persistent, more faithful—remain
for a long time, like souls, recalling, waiting, hoping,
upon the ruin of all the rest, containing in their nearly
impalpable droplet, the immense edifice of memory.

— Marcel Proust, *In Search of Lost Time*

1

Souvenir

HANDS DOWN MY FAVORITE HEIST EVER.

It started innocently enough. I'd been recruited to accompany a tour group in the Dordogne Valley, and my job consisted of giving a few lectures about life in France. The rest of the time, my wife, Anne, and I traipsed along with the herd of three dozen Americans. The local guide was a forty-something woman whose wardrobe still clung to her twenties. Marie-Laure's long scarf flowed behind her as she steered the group through quaint downtowns filled with replicas of ancient buildings. We tasted walnut oil and examined pots, admired endless churches with banks of stained glass. The tour specialized in the picturesque, and our dark-haired leader knew just what to show Americans. In the coach she whispered to the bus driver about where to pull over for the next photo op, and at the chateau she corralled everyone toward the west tower, the one they *had* to see. We traveled from postcard to postcard, and I lapped it up with everyone else.

Then came the evening they planted us in front of two hours of folkloric dance, performed by grim-faced locals in knickers and suspenders. The applause was thunderous, and for once people got to call out *encore!* in the country that invented the term. After the show I chatted with one of the curly-haired dancers. While he sucked on a cigarette, I asked if they performed very often. He glanced around to make sure his boss was out of earshot. "Nah," he said. He let the smoke stream from his nostrils. "We just do this shit for the tourists."

I felt like a kid in Disneyland who bumps into Mickey on a cigarette break, the mouse head pulled off.

Something was going on.

"Relax already," Anne said when I told her about it. "Kick back and enjoy yourself."

I tried. I went with the group to Lascaux, where we stood in line to stare at a modern reproduction of a prehistoric cave. One afternoon we had a wine tasting. And a cheese tasting. And a chocolate tasting. The weather seemed made to order, the dial locked on *pleasantly warm.*

Then, in Sarlat, a man in our group wandered off down a side street, and Marie-Laure chased him down like a border collie. What didn't she want him to see? I couldn't shake the sense that there was a seam somewhere, the edge of a stage set.

It all came to a head the day they brought us to the goose farm. As we hiked across the field to an outbuilding, I nudged Anne, lifted a foot, and pointed at the sole of my shoe.

"What?" she said.

"See?"

"See *what?* There's nothing there."

I nodded vigorously. "Exactly. A farm with no shit."

Her eye-roll was interrupted by the arrival of those escorting us into yesteryear. There was a smiling man in pristine overalls, a beret screwed to his head—along with his father, hands knotted, trousers filthy, a sullen and wrinkled representative of tradition. The son, Martin, greeted us and trotted out a few jokes. He winked at Marie-Laure and twirled an imaginary moustache, suggesting an amorous relationship.

"Yoo know 'ow we men are een France!" he quipped. The accent verged on outrageous.

Everyone laughed.

Behind him, the father, who was staring at nothing, went gray in the face. His shoulders rounded even more.

The visit got underway. Step by step we learned how they turned birds into little cans of foie gras, the kind awaiting our arrival in the gift shop. There was all the breeding and brooding, the great out-of-doors, and the free range. Eventually Martin eased into the gruesome part that is hard to sugar-coat, the bit about shoving a funnel into the goose's gullet and pouring in the grain.

"But *non*, do not worry," Martin chuckled as he pantomimed the feeding. "Zee goose, he don't really mind! He ees a 'ungry bugger, zee goose! He weel take all yoo can geeve!

The laughter turned to guffaws. With jolliness and a few exaggerated shrugs, Martin had turned goose torture into a knee-slapper.

In the background, the silent father, a reluctant extra in this performance, had gone ashen. What wouldn't he have given to be elsewhere—indeed, *anywhere* other than here, in front of a gawking audience demanding that saucy Frenchness be enacted before them?

And that's when the penny dropped. No, it wasn't just the geese who were being fattened up for slaughter. It was *us*, the Americans. For the past ten days the tour operator had stuck a funnel in our brains and was pouring in the clichés, gallon after gallon. Like the geese, we didn't even object. The more they gave us, the more we swallowed. Gluttons for this particular punishment, we were insatiable.

I don't believe I've ever had such a sad realization. Everyone we'd encountered over the past week was complicit in the scam—the vendors, the tour guides, the hoteliers, the waiters, and, indeed, even the victims, who—myself included—wanted nothing more than to be duped and beguiled. We wanted the pretty stuff. Like spoiled kids at the dinner table, we demanded dessert while refusing to eat our vegetables. But because we were kids with credit cards, they gave us what we thought we wanted.

On the ride back to the hotel, I stared blankly out the window as blurred countryside rolled by. Anne tried to buck me up, which somehow made it worse.

All the others climbed off the bus before I could struggle to my feet, and then I stood outside the reception area, a bit dazed, not sure which way to go. Why bother?

Everyone else had dashed off to put away their cameras and their goose paraphernalia before heading out to dinner.

That's when the first cry erupted from the hotel. It was a woman's voice, high-pitched and startled. Another woman responded, calling out something in English. A man joined in. Then the footsteps began to thunder. Members of our group were scurrying back and forth in the corridors, thumping on doors, checking on their friends. Were they OK? Had their room been broken into as well?

A heist!

The rest was like a waking dream, the scenes flowing together. Outraged Americans mobbed the front desk. The manager with slicked-back hair literally wrung his hands. Marie-Laure ran this way, then that, flummoxed by this event that hadn't figured on the itinerary. Finally, a siren sounded, and a little green car screeched to a stop out front, a troupe of gendarmes tumbling out of it.

While we were away, someone had gone through the hotel and ripped the wall safes from the wardrobes in the bedrooms. Wallets had vanished, jewelry, even passports!

How would we pay for our meals? What did we need for insurance? Who knew how to fill out a French police report? What if—and now people started eyeing the staff—it was an inside job?

Just like that, the postcard of our French experience had been ripped asunder.

Anne glanced at me and did a double-take. "What's up with you?" she said. "You're beaming."

She was right. I was imagining the grandpa at the goose farm—how he'd have relished this scene. Life was just too wonderful. Oh, sure, we'd lost a few bucks. There'd be insurance claims to file. But better than any souvenir, we'd finally been granted something real and unreproducible—a genuine memory.

The gendarmes were now frisking the chambermaids, one by one.

Anne began to giggle, covering her mouth. While pandemonium swirled around us, the snorts erupted, her laughter fueling mine, mine turbo-boosting hers.

"Oh my God," she said, wiping a tear from her cheek. "This is one is for the books. I'm going to remember it forever."

Yep, I thought, drunk with happiness. Me too. Forever.

That was so many years ago.

Only problem is, forever never lasts as long as you think it will. Back then I didn't know how time passes. How the future creeps up on you. And how sometimes, when you look over your shoulder at yesteryear, what was supposed to be forever has faded from sight.

2

Memory

WHICH IS, AFTER ALL, what the word *souvenir* means. You hear it all the time in France. *Je me souviens*, someone murmurs over a glass of wine, and you know you're about to get a dose of the past. *Souviens-toi!* a mother warns her kid, telling him not to forget. And all those trinkets collected when we travel? They're doing the same thing, whispering reminders in our ears.

My first mementos from Paris live in a shoe box in my closet, and they date back to the year of the Family Trip when I was ten. God knows what possessed Mom and Dad to drag a family of six from Minnesota over to the City of Light. The tattered remains of that failed expedition include a cardboard map from our cruise down the Seine on a Bateau Mouche and a medallion with a hawk-nosed profile of Napoleon. There's a used Metro ticket in that box, too, along with a couple of postcards.

But my prized possession is a mass-produced, four-inch-tall Eiffel Tower, purchased for six or seven francs—the entirety of my young fortune.

The thing about souvenirs is that each one is half-junk, half-heirloom. Eiffel Towers are cranked out by the millions in Shanghai or Guangzhou, and each one resembles its gigantic ancestor. But mine is imprinted with a specific memory. It recalls our family ascent as we stood packed like cigarettes in that elevator, and it bears the trace of the high wind as we exited, the planks beneath our feet, the view of infinity from the railing. A whole scene blooms from that crusty souvenir, like the genie from Aladdin's lamp: the overpriced ice cream cones we talked our parents into buying, the coins we dropped into the mounted telescope—and then, in a culmination of smooth-talking, my brother and I extracted permission to descend from the second story by way of the metal stairs that zigzag down the leg of the Iron Lady.

How we bounded, taking the steps by threes and fours, wheeling around landings, swirling down thirty or forty flights, until finally we halted to catch our breath, convinced we were nearly there—only to look out and see that somehow, incredibly, the ant-people below were just as small as before.

One of the great pleasures in life comes when you get to share your shoebox of souvenirs with another person. That's how it went with Anne, back when we first started coming for long stays in this blasted country. As newlyweds, we spent a summer working as grunt laborers in a chateau in the Loire Valley. That's where we started collecting memories of our own. The family running the place was noble but penniless, doing everything they could to make a franc. While Anne ironed endless sheets in the failing bed-and-breakfast enterprise, I worked the fields, herding sheep and tinkering with machinery. They'd turned the grounds into a place to manufacture dried flowers, and the operation was run by an impetuous aristocrat named François who specialized in harebrained schemes—like the one that had us load two tons of blossoms into a lumber kiln for drying. We scooped up the cinders the next day.

During that summer I spent a full week on my hands and knees behind a Massey-Ferguson tractor as we scraped up tulip bulbs with our bare hands. I started chatting with my neighbor, as you do.

"*Ça va?*" I said.

"*Oui, thah va,*" he replied.

I thought it was maybe a regional accent, but it turned out he had a lisp. We yakked as we sank our hands into the dirt, fishing for bulbs. I learned he was a member of the family. Also an aristocrat. A viscount. Whatever that is.

I stood up and introduced myself, and he did the same, holding out a muddy hand to shake.

"Scott," I said.

"*Thavier,*" he replied.

"*Pardon?*"

"*Thavier.*"

He meant Xavier.

I took it in. Here I was on the grounds of a French chateau, my new wife cleaning the semen stains of guests out of the laundry while I harvested tulip bulbs next to a viscount who was burdened with a name he couldn't pronounce.

The word for this: *un souvenir*. Into the shoebox it went.

Anne and I traveled about for a while, working and living in the provinces. But like iron filings, we eventually got pulled to the magnet—ending up in Paris. I'd not really spent much time in the capital since buying my Eiffel Tower decades earlier, but faster than you could say *sacré bleu* we were putting the kids in daycare, then the schools. We bought an apartment in the thirteenth arrondissement, embedding ourselves in a neighborhood that smacked of life.

I wasn't so good at keeping track of the present—let alone the past—so I outsourced the task of remembering to Anne. This was her forte. She pasted photos in albums, kept a journal. She knew who was who. Years went by, and memories piled up like all those tchotchkes in my grandma's knickknack cabinet—and like Grandma, Anne could always find the one she wanted.

It took a while, but soon I realized that Paris is altogether different from the rest of France on the *souvenir* front. It's like thinking you know what oranges are, and then you visit Florida. Nobody does memory-making like the City of Light. It's their specialty.

This city is so memorable that people have recollections of it before they even get here. In everyone's brain there lives a collage made from movies and advertisements and perfumes and luxury handbags and bulldogs and go-get-'em girls named Emily. No one rolls into this town for the first time, jabs a finger toward the tower looming over the skyline, and says, *What the hell is that thing?* Long before the tires hit the tarmac at Charles-de-Gaulle, visitors know exactly what they're coming for—romance, fashion, grandeur. Even those rude waiters (disappointingly hard to find these days) are part of the hallucination. It's the funnel in the goose's mouth, all over again. And they've got a lot of grain to pour in.

Which is what brought to mind that heist, all those years ago, in the hotel in Dordogne. What a gift that had been! It was the kind of thing that made you want to train as a cat burglar, but one with a special MO, one where you steal people's costume jewelry, replacing it with real diamonds. What I wanted to do was purloin all the clichés about Paris, while giving people something more valuable—a set of unreproducible experiences, otherwise known as *reality*.

It would be easier pull off that kind of trick if people had never heard of Paris before coming here. Then their minds would be a vacant lot, and you could just frame up their vision, wall by wall, from the ground up. Unfortunately, when it comes to the City of Light, you're stuck with one of those awful remodeling jobs—the kind where you can't build anything until you've knocked down the ramshackle mess the previous contractor left you with. Which is tough, because folks have gotten used to that mess. They actually like it.

My first attempt at the reconstruction was a book called *French Like Moi*, where I poked the bear. It did pretty well. But some readers were scandalized. *This book was totally worthless*, one reader sputtered in her review. *It didn't help a whit during our trip to Paris!* And she wasn't wrong. After all, I'd neglected to include a single pastry flake of useful information. People want to know how to buy Metro tickets and where to find the Champs Elysées. They're dying to know why the Mona Lisa is so pleased with herself.

Another reader complained that I'd "ruined" Paris by talking about the seedy parts, the underbelly, the armpits of the city. I'd shown things people weren't supposed to see.

The more I thought about it, the more I realized that France is like *The Matrix*—a world of make-believe that passes itself off as the real thing. It's a grab-bag of berets and baguettes and poodles and small café tables with checkered tablecloths, long-legged women and narrow-hipped paramours. Who would want to interrupt such a great dream? Imagine that someone stomps in and invites you to choose between the red pill and the blue one. If you choose red, it tastes icky and is hard to swallow, and you won't like what you see when you wake up. Go for blue, and it'll be Disneyland forever.

Yes, please!

In addition to all the memories you arrive with, weighing you down like oversized suitcases, the city churns out additional memorable moments during your stay. Every street corner is photogenic, every cobblestone triggers a sigh. And should you run short of memories of your own, tons of pre-made ones are available for purchase. By the time you return home, you find yourself overloaded with mementos. And like that stain on your shirt from the last steak-frites, you can't wash them away, because the essence of this city is that it's unforgettable.

As Rick tells Ilsa in *Casablanca*, when everything else is falling apart, "We'll always have Paris."

Until we don't.

Anne and I had been coming for decades, living here for a year at a time. Half of our life was now in France. It had been glorious enough, as these things go. But then a few of the tchotchkes started going missing.

At first I thought they'd just been misplaced. Anne couldn't come up with someone's name. A word danced at the tip of her tongue, refusing to make its grand entrance. Soon enough, though, there was more. The shopping list gave her trouble. She made mistakes counting out money. Words eluded her. In the neighborhood, she got so turned around that even the landmark of the Great Public Toilet no longer helped.

Her problem? It was the very thing Paris specialized in: *souvenirs*, memories.

The doctor visits started. GPs. Neurologists. Technicians. Life turned into a series of acronyms—MRIs, PETs, ADLs....

What she suffered from was the big A, that form of dementia for which useful meds were pretty much DOA or AWOL.

And yet, Anne still loved the city. But her perimeter shrank. The pills—neither red nor blue, as it happened—didn't help. You could see the change month by month. The word for it was *precipitous*. And yet she still somehow managed. It was the Eiffel Tower effect all over again: you can go down really fast, but when you start from such a high elevation, it takes a long time to get to the bottom.

I took on the role of caregiver, preparing mostly edible meals and tackling the laundry. I ironed the sheets the way she used to at the chateau. By this point, the kids had flown the coop, Paul working in New York, Muriel at college in Pennsylvania. They came back so often that the dad in me would sometimes have to chase them away from their mom's shrinking present so they could develop their own budding futures.

Bit by bit, pages vanished from our mental album. Whole stories were lost. Anne began to fade—not because I'd left her, but because she was leaving me, bit by memorial bit. It was like that caper in the hotel in Sarlat. Someone was stealing her away.

A few years passed like this, and I became a widower-in-training. Paris started to feel haunted in an anticipatory way. I'd turn a corner in the city and stumble upon the playground where we used to take the kids—who, at this point, were young adults she barely recognized. The very sight of her

favorite park reminded me that she'd forgotten it. The supermarket had become a labyrinth. Even the apartment called
to mind a past that for one of us was no longer tethered.

In *French Like Moi*, I wrote about the catacombs that riddle the left bank of the city, endless and empty passageways
where the bedrock has been extracted. That's what the surface felt like these days, or how I felt, myself—a place where
something used to be, like the dusty spot on the floor after
the sofa is moved. What, I started wondering, were we even
doing here anymore? The city had given us much in the past,
but now I craved something more or different. I wasn't sure
Paris could still deliver.

Life with Anne was becoming smaller and quieter. In
the evening she liked to play a version of gin rummy where
I organized her hand and pretended to be surprised by what
she discarded. She had a favorite movie that we watched
again and again. She exclaimed with surprise at each turn in
the plot, although she'd seen it all before.

There was no point. And that's when I decided to sell
the apartment.

The notary explained all the options, and soon I found
myself staring at a sheaf of documents on my desk. That's
how things go. You get older and you prepare your exit. You
put the house on the market, and people come to examine
your walls with hungry eyes. The page of generations turns.

I took a walk to think it all over. What would it mean, to
no longer live above that bakery? Would I miss the vagrants

who hang out on the bench? What about the church, the one where pieces of plaster rained down on parishioners? Down at the corner, workers in yellow vests were jackhammering the sidewalk again, and a maniac on a city bike careened through pedestrians. You couldn't deny it was a bit of a mess.

But it was *my* mess, kind of. At least, it used to be.

When I returned home, two women were grousing in the entryway. There was Danielle, the silver-haired retiree who serves with me on the building committee, along with Mme Estevès, the new concierge. Was that smoke coming out of their ears? Danielle, spitting mad, pointed down the hallway while Mme Estevès raised her arms to the heavens.

Something had happened.

They turned to me as I approached, and words hailed down like plaster from the church ceiling. I made out a few chunks of their outrage—"*un étron... local poubelles... humain... inadmissible!*"

The translation: A human turd had been found on the floor of the garbage area.

Their rants of indignation faded to the background as warmth radiated through my chest. I'd been touched by grace.

The curtain was rising on the stage of life. A show was about to begin. Even or especially in the midst of tragedy, don't you need a bit of fun?

What the hell. There was no rush to put the place up for sale. I decided to give Paris a second chance.

After all, this new adventure promised to be *memorable*.

3

Le Turd

In the Midwest, if a tornado rips through town at a weird time of year, people scratch their head, trying to figure out if it's an isolated incident or the start of a new trend—just bad weather or climate change. That was the question in our apartment building in Paris the day the concierge found a human turd in the garbage area. Was it a one-off, or was this the new normal?

Let me explain. Our building is an eight-story affair located on the rue Bobillot in the thirteenth arrondissement. It's a 1930s structure with a vibe of Art Deco done on the cheap. The place is low-security by Parisian standards, but you do have to pass through two code-locked doors to make it into the hallway. That means we are rarely surprised by what we encounter on the premises. I once found a copy of *Robinson Crusoe* abandoned on the radiator by the stairs, and occasionally Madame Estevès, the concierge, leaves a mop in a corner. But outsiders can't easily dump leftover furniture or dead bodies here. As for defecation, the human variety has traditionally been restricted to private areas. (Some years ago there'd been an issue with the canine variant, but the infamous woman of the fifth floor, *la dame du cinquième*, had since moved away.)

But then came the day I found Danielle and Madame Estevès in a heated discussion in French, and I learned that someone had taken a dump in the room where we keep the building's garbage cans. The two women were outraged. Who had ever heard of such a thing? This was beyond the pale!

"Are you sure it's real?" I asked.

They gaped at me. Mme Estevès mostly speaks Portuguese, so I figured she hadn't understood. As for Danielle, her hearing isn't what it used to be. But then they looked at each other and rolled their eyes in unison, and I could practically hear their shared thought: stupid American. Danielle dragged me to the doorway of the garbage room—known as the *local poubelles*—and pointed. I conducted my inspection from a distance. It was the real McCoy all right. Not coiled, the way they make the fake ones, but long and dark, with a banana-like curve to it. I'm not sure what the standard measurements are for these things, but I pegged it as an XL.

What were we going to do about it, that's what Danielle wanted to know.

"Maybe throw it away?" I suggested. After all, the garbage cans were right there.

But she was more inclined toward a declaration of war.

Danielle is the only member of our building committee who's retired, so even though she's not the one we elected president, everyone knows she's really in charge, rather like Dick Cheney during the Bush years.

Her finger drove into the air. "I shall call a meeting."

I confess I hesitated to bring Anne into the loop of this little drama. After all, she had her hands full just keeping reality from floating off every day, and I figured the story of a turd appearing in the *local poubelles* wasn't likely to command the attention it might otherwise deserve.

Boy, was I wrong.

She heard me chatting with Danielle, and before I could stop myself, I'd spilled the beans. She listened without blinking, taking it all in. In the old days she would have shrugged it off, but the new Anne was fascinated. Here was a woman who couldn't remember how she'd spent the last fifteen minutes, but somehow this tale stuck. It confirmed my hunch that emotion is the mortar that cements memories in place.

After learning about the turd, she'd pass by neighbors in the hallway and whisper to me, a little too loudly—"Did he do it? No? What about that one?"

Our building contains some fifty units, including the shops on the ground floor. We work with a management company run by the eagle-eyed Madame Lesur, but actual decisions are made by the *conseil syndical*, which sounds prestigious, like the Council of Trent, but is really just six of the condo owners—the ones who failed to step backward when volunteers were sought at the *assemblée générale*, or annual meeting. We used to gather regularly to ponder the building's welfare, but since the completion of some of the larger projects, we mostly wait for Danielle to send out the bat signal.

Danielle lives just down the hallway, and her two-room apartment reminds me of the "tiny house" movement in the US, filled as it is with doll-sized furniture and clever, space-saving contraptions. But because her father was a sculptor, the place also serves as a miniature museum, one displaying more amorphous, nude women than you typically expect to encounter in someone's living room.

As the group huddled around the doily-covered table that evening, we began with our traditional throat-clearing, where everyone complains about serving on the committee. I grumble along with the rest of them, doing my best to sound irritated. The fact is, though, that I live for the *conseil syndical*. For someone as enamored as I am of petty dramas, this committee is the goose that lays the golden eggs. Every few months a new dilemma would plop out of the cloaca of the *conseil syndical*, and we'd be charged with figuring out who had made unauthorized modifications, who left personal effects in the common spaces, who was lagging in payment of their fees, and what to do about it all. Each one had the contours of a story.

Danielle recounted the event that caused us to convene, and I chimed in, offering details about position, color, and odor. Around the table, lips curled. Hélène, usually so poised, winced her eyes shut, as though to avoid seeing an object that was not currently there. Madeleine, more unbridled, let fly with a squawk of indignation.

Skinny Cyril is a theater director in real life, but his expression of disgust suggested he had failed to latch onto the dramatic potential of our little whodunit.

"Well," said Franck, lifting up his beefy palms in a sign of surrender, "I'm the new one here, so I'll let all of you decide what to do." He'd moved in just a couple months ago. With his remodeling project underway, he was playing an *I'm too busy* card.

After the preliminaries, we settled into the investigatory phase, which I thought of as *CSI: Bobillot*. Problem was—and this is true of so many procedurals early in an episode—we were short on evidence. At this point, the "body" had already been disposed of by the concierge, and we didn't have so much as a chalk outline of where it had been.

"Well," I said, "at least we know it was a guy."

Eyebrows went up around the table.

"I mean," I began, "I suppose it *could* have been a woman. I'm just thinking about the... the..." And suddenly I realized I wasn't sure what term to use for the girth of a turd, in any language. The word that eventually came out of my mouth was *gabarit*, which is mostly reserved for describing the breadth of a motor vehicle. It made quite an impression.

Still, without the tools to undertake any real forensics, we turned our attention to things that might be considered circumstantial or hypothetical, or possibly speculative.

Some years ago the son of one of the residents had drawn a profile of male genitals on the wall of the elevator. Might he have returned from college to reprise his shenanigans? Or what if a homeless person had come in and spent the night in the *local poubelles*?

Then Madeleine stood up at the table and tossed her scarf over her shoulder, commanding our attention. Wasn't it just possible that the crime had been committed *elsewhere*, and that the "body" had been moved to the location where we'd found it?

That one blew our minds.

Problem is, nothing made sense. We figured it had to be an outside job, for what resident would come all the way downstairs to lay one out among the garbage cans when they had perfectly functioning facilities right at home? On the other hand, why would anyone creep into our building to do their business there, given that right outside, on the square, there stood the far more appealing public toilet? And on the third hand, how could an outsider even make it through the front doors, secured by those passcodes?

The whole thing reminded me of that Poe story where they discover that an inscrutable murder was committed by an orangutan. I don't know much about the stools of various primates, but it seemed as likely a solution as anything else we were considering.

All in all, we were left with a cold case, and our little group disbanded without taking any action. Maybe we didn't need to panic. A single turd does not a trend make. For the moment, it was like that one-off funnel cloud in the Midwest—just weather.

Or was it climate change?

It's funny how fast the human brain sees what it wants to see. I don't know who first looked at the night sky and made dot-to-dot pictures of it, but it's pretty clear they fudged the evidence to find things that weren't there. In our case, we were hoping to find nothing at all, and the longer there was nothing to find, the more we allowed ourselves to hope it would continue. The whole thing reminded me of winters as a kid, when the skating pond would freeze over and people would inch out onto the new ice, tapping to make sure it was thick enough to bear their weight. They'd tiptoe around for a minute, give it a bounce or two, and soon be stomping and sliding, throwing caution to the wind. But then someone would break through and be up to their hips in ice water.

I think that's how it generally goes with people. We're so eager for the ice of life to support our weight that we fool ourselves rather quickly into believing that it will.

At first, the six of us who knew the secret—seven, if you count Madame Estevès—were waddling about as if we were testing the ice. Then, after a couple of days, we gained a bit more confidence, and soon the spring had returned to our step. Phew! The danger was past!

Until Danielle knocked at my door one morning.

"There's another one," she seethed.

At first I didn't know what she was talking about. Did she mean another American had moved into the building?

"*Un deuxième!*" she added.

Anne and I already counted as two, so it wasn't that.

Then I understood.

I traipsed downstairs. Would it be in the entryway this time? On the steps to the cellar? Nope. The crime scene was once again the *local poubelles*. The "corpse" lay in roughly the same position as the first victim. I wouldn't call this one its twin, but I figured it was a close relative, judging by the width of its chassis.

I'd been in this building for seventeen years without once encountering a single crime of this nature, and now we'd had two in a span of ten days. No doubt about it, we had a serial crapper on our hands.

An emergency meeting was called.

There are some sixty or seventy people living in our building at any given moment, and if you include all those with access to the door codes—say, the mailman, two or three delivery people, and the 800,000 friends and relatives who occasionally come by—you're left with a wide field of suspects. Profiling the culprit would require us to speculate about means, motive, and opportunity. Problem was, pretty much everyone had the means—that is, unless some of the residents had had their bowels resected. And opportunity didn't do much to narrow the focus either. Not even the "time of death" could be calculated, for no one had volunteered to take the temperature of the corpse. All we knew was that the dirty work happened at night, which left a pretty broad window.

The remaining category was thus motive, but that stumped us, too. Madeleine suggested it might be some sort of protest. Hélène thought it could be a compulsive behavior by someone who couldn't help himself. I liked to think it was a kind of gift, provided to stir our imagination, rather like that monolith in the movie *2001*.

"I don't know," Franck said in his barrel-chested voice. "I'm the new one here, but maybe someone just really had to go."

That theory was shot down by Danielle. "There's a WC available in the same hallway!" she cried.

Which was true. On the ground floor there is an unmarked washroom with a toilet, mostly used by the shopkeepers, but officially available to everyone in the building. It wasn't even ten paces past the *local poubelles*. Which meant one of two things. Theory Number One ran that our mystery guest was so close to exploding that he couldn't make it the last few steps to the bathroom. But that seemed inconsistent with the well-formed and solid nature of the deposit.

So it had to be Theory Number Two: whoever it was *really* wanted to make a point.

Finding the guilty party was going to take a while, and in the meantime, we needed to defend ourselves. There was discussion of putting a lock on the door to the garbage can area, but of course, people had to be able to drop off their trash, which meant we'd end up giving everyone a key, which rather defeated the purpose.

Then Cyril's eyes half-closed, catlike. An idea was blooming under that balding scalp of his. The reason our pool of suspects was so large, he said, was because half the city had our door codes. If we changed those codes, sharing the new ones only with the building residents, we would instantly bar entry to outsiders, which would either exclude our culprit, thereby solving our problem, or else reveal him to be in our midst. If the offense was repeated after the lockdown, it could only be by one of our neighbors.

A hush settled over the group. It's not often you find yourself in the presence of genius, and we gave Cyril his due.

I was the one who met with the locksmith two days later. He plodded back and forth, opening this panel and that. While he fiddled, I confided to him why we were making the change, expecting a reaction of disgust or even outrage.

"You don't say," he replied in a world-weary tone. He was a locksmith in Paris. He had seen everything.

Twenty minutes later, it was done. The new codes were in place, and soon the residents had been informed. For a few days, even the mailman couldn't get in.

Our vigil began.

Anne remained fascinated with what I'd come to call Turd-Gate. During the previous weeks she had spent a good deal of time in front of the TV watching larvae pupate and unfold into butterflies, or cheetahs picking off gazelles. But there was no way the natural world could compete with the high drama unfolding in the rue Bobillot. Problem was, she'd gone fuzzy on the details. Had there been one turd or several? Had they been in our building, or somewhere else? On our way to the park, every passerby looked shady, and she viewed our outings as one long police lineup, confiding her suspicions to me as we walked. The more you look at Parisians, the more you feel they have something to hide. Many of them skulk. They make furtive glances. Like all of us, they're certainly guilty of something.

Anne's constant accusation of those around us began to stoke my own paranoia. It's a terrible thing to study your neighbors and wonder which of them is a monster, but once the boulder of suspicion gets rolling, it's hard to stop it. Madame Estevès's cleanup duties put her beyond reproach, but what about that teenage girl on the seventh floor? Could she possibly have produced such a specimen? Or the withered old guy on the sixth? How about the mysterious doctor on the ground floor—the one no one ever saw in person?

Then a new thought dawned on me. What if the wolf were not disguised among the sheep, but actually among the shepherds? By which I meant, *what about...the conseil syndical itself?* It made perfect sense. Danielle could have done it, or Madeleine, or Cyril, or Hélène. Or—and this felt right—what about Franck? He was the new one on our council, with that remodeling project. What if he'd forgotten to install a toilet?

I shook it off. No, we'd do better with the orang-utan theory.

Or perhaps no theory at all. While I'd been working myself into a lather, the pooping had ground to a halt. Changing the door codes seemed to have done the trick. The *local poubelles* resumed its function as a depository for waste that was not, strictly speaking, human.

Anne seemed disappointed at this turn of events, but she got it—all good things come to an end.

Then came the bat signal, pinging in my inbox. Emergency meeting. No agenda.

By the time I made it to Danielle's, everyone else was huddled around her little dining room table.

"*Qu'est-ce qui se passe?*" I asked, lifting my palms in a whazzup sort of way.

"There's another one!" Danielle hissed in French. "*Le troisième!*" Then, perhaps to emphasize the enormity of it, she repeated herself in English for the benefit of the American in the room. However, because French people struggle to make the *t-h* sound, instead of referring to "the third," she pronounced it "*zee turd.*"

From the mouths of aging babes.

The details spilled out. Nearly two weeks had gone by since we barred entry to outsiders, but now a new delivery had been made. Unless there'd been some unauthorized broadcast of the passcodes (or a recent migration of orang-utans to the neighborhood), we had to face the facts: the culprit was among us.

What to do? The police aren't interested in penny-ante crime. Posting warnings on the front door wasn't likely to have an effect. Franck mentioned the option of dusting for fingerprints, but who in our building would not have left traces on the doorknob of the *local poubelles*, the only space that every single resident visited on a regular basis? DNA testing would have been possible, but no one wanted to swab their neighbors.

We traipsed downstairs to the crime scene, lest some shred of evidence had been overlooked. You never know when a fraternity ring or a fiber from a lapel might have escaped notice. Danielle explained where the latest stiff had been found—in the corner, behind the yellow recycling bin and one of the green garbage cans. Uncharacteristically, our crapper seemed to have gone for a smidgen of privacy.

"How did you even see it?" Hélène asked.

It was a good question.

Danielle gave a falsely humble shrug. "*J'ai l'oeil américain*."

Having the American eye is a dusty old expression in French. It means that nothing gets past you—you catch it all. The idiom dates back to some earlier age, when Americans could be counted on to detect the glint of a six-shooter coming out of its holster, or a fifth ace in a deck of cards. These days, of course, most Americans don't bother noticing much at all. I myself have outsourced the job of paying attention to things. For example, I'm altogether in favor of self-driving cars since I'm so easily distracted, and if the garage door opener of my American home didn't have an electric eye, I'd have long ago chopped myself in two with the thing. Moreover, I plan to buy one of those doorbells that show who's at the door so you know when to pretend you're not home.

It was that last thought—the idea of watching people from a distance—that caused lightning to strike.

"What we need," I proclaimed, "is a surveillance camera."

I have to say, I felt pretty pleased with myself. It was the perfect solution. Already I could see how Danielle would spend her evenings, squinting at grainy footage of the *local poubelles* on a monitor, knitting fiercely. When we hauled the culprit into court, a bewigged lawyer would project the crime on a giant screen. They'd freeze it on a single frame, and the lawyer would call for it to be enlarged, and then enhanced. A murmur would run through the courtroom as we identified the culprit lowering his *pantalon*. Even though France retired the guillotine in 1981, they'd pull it out of mothballs for this. Thanks to the unblinking eye of a surveillance camera, we'd all get to see the guilty party carted in a tumbril to the Place de la Concorde as the masses screamed for justice.

To think that it took an American to figure this out!

I awaited their expressions of gratitude—not applause necessarily, but maybe a low whistle of admiration, an ahhh or two. The silence stretched.

"We can't do that!" Madeleine finally spat.

"Definitely not," confirmed Hélène.

Franck and Danielle were scandalized. Cyril looked if he no longer recognized me.

It turns out I'd tripped over one of those invisible thresholds separating French and American culture, and it took me a while to put it all together.

In the US, we each have a lot of rights, and we don't like them being trampled—not by the government, or by woo-woo organizations, or, especially, by other people, whose rights are by definition less important than our own. It's true we don't agree on the details—whether the arms we get to bear should be pellet guns or AR-15s, or how much of your neighbor's body should be under your control, but we defend these rights fiercely. Indeed, I have often thought that the national motto *E pluribus unum* should be replaced by whatever the Latin is for *Don't fuck with my stuff*.

All that said, Americans have pretty much thrown in the towel on one thing—the right to privacy. Unless you're making mega-donations to a Super-Pac, it's hard to stay out of the limelight. Scammers have ready access to your phone number and email, the supermarket tracks your diet, and website cookies cobble together a 3-D replica of you for the sake of marketers. They say that walls have ears, but so, somehow, does Google. A month ago, I was talking about a friend who'd recently died, and the next day ads for funeral homes were clogging my phone. Welcome to the new normal.

But here on the rue Bobillot, I was confronted with a different mindset.

In France it may be considered impolite to take a dump in someone else's *local poubelles*, but at least you can expect a little peace and quiet while you do it. It's the same reason they're always hauling Facebook into court here, and popping up those annoying permissions on websites. In short, privacy is still a thing in these parts. It may seem quaint, but people's personal lives remain shrouded in mystery, and a host of laws governs the collection of data. A few years ago, the President of the Republic was filmed escaping from the Elysée Palace on a moped to visit his mistress, and the ensuing hue and cry focused less on the infidelity and the breach of security protocols than on how the press had peeked into his private life.

Surely, the *conseil syndical* seemed to suggest, a turd deserved the same protections.

It wasn't long before I hit upon a fallback plan. We could install a *fake* camera, so that the crapper only *thought* he was being filmed, which would encourage him to do his business elsewhere. I found this to be the perfect compromise— the American threat of the all-seeing eye, joined with the French promise of blindness.

But no, that too was shot down. Even pretending to invade someone's privacy was a bridge too far. The one person in our group who might legitimately claim to possess an American eye revealed himself to be a bit short-sighted.

So, what was it—weather or climate change? And if the latter, what on earth could we do to reverse it? Perhaps we'd already gone past the tipping point, and our future held a never-ending crescendo of bigger and messier cataclysms.

In the end, it was Danielle who came up with the solution. The next day she toddled off to the little shoe-repair shop that's just down the street. These mom-and-pop establishments will happily re-sole your boots, but they also run a sideline in key-cutting and sign-making. The next time I descended to the *local poubelles* to drop off my recycling, a small metal plate had been affixed to the wall near the door. In elegant gold letters there stood the word *toilettes*. A line at the bottom ended with an arrow that pointed down the hallway, in the direction of the little washroom.

I can't say the mystery was truly solved, but it did come to an end. The corpses by the garbage cans were over, and life on the rue Bobillot returned to normal. Anne went back to watching nature programs.

But in my daydreams, I imagine that the culprit really was an orangutan—and that, because we're in Paris, that great, enlightened center of learning, even the apes know how to read a sign and follow an arrow.

4

Fake-It-and-Wait

I FOUND HER STANDING BEFORE the shelves in the bedroom, rows of titles staring back.

"Whatchya looking for?" I asked.

"The book," Anne said.

"Which one?"

"The one for…you know…for finding…words."

I got it. Her French had always been shaky, and with her illness, words were trickling away. I located the French-English dictionary on the bottom shelf and held it out.

"No," she said. "Not that one. The other."

Which is when I realized she was talking about English.

She'd reached the point in her disease where plenty of definitions still rolled around in her head, but the labels eluded her—little things like the kind of food she wanted, or the names of our kids, or the three nouns the neurologist gave her every few months to test her memory. The connection between words and things came and went, and sometimes the wires got crossed. Though she'd taught English for thirty years, her grammar had gone wonky. A dictionary might help pin things down.

The situation reminded me of an interaction I'd had a few weeks earlier, at the Bricorama hardware store.

"I'm looking..." I'd said to a yellow-vested employee named Jérôme, "for a...kind of...you know...a sort of...a *thing*...." I didn't have the words, and the more I struggled in the other man's language, the smaller his eyes went. I'd been frequenting this shop for the past decade, but the staff still hadn't learned how to read my mind.

My next step was pantomime—one hand covering the other fist, twisting as though screwing a cap on a jar. "You know...one that will let me tighten...the other...thing...on the top of the toilet."

Finally Jérôme's head rolled back and he emitted a long *ah*, the universal sign for *I have had a minor epiphany*.

"Yes, yes," he announced flatly in French. "You're looking for an *egrudecouleau*."

"A what?"

I recognized the look in his eyes. It was the same one people leveled at Anne when they caught on that something wasn't quite right. My incomprehension implied a problem of the cognitive sort. He broke it down into bite-sized portions. "An *e-gru-de-cou-leau*. Over there. Aisle 13."

Egrudecouleau, I hasten to explain, is not a word in any language, past or present. But that's what it sounded like. I suppose I could have asked again, striving for clarification, but too much time had passed. I'd reached that fork in the conversational road where a man has to choose between forging ahead and confessing his ignorance.

"Of course," I said, thanking him profusely before toddling off to the longest aisle in the store, the one filled with several hundred doohickeys and thingamajigs. If I spent the rest of the day picking through shrink-wrapped packets, there was a non-zero chance I might actually locate what I needed, and in the process would discover the word Jérôme had uttered—assuming it appeared on the packaging. Most importantly, my honor would remain intact.

I began my search.

I have no problem confessing that I struggle with math or that I can't pry the child-proof cover off a pill bottle. But when it comes to words, I feel I'm supposed to know what I'm doing. As far as hardware stores go, I chalk it up to my dad, who grew up in a small town, spending time on the family farm. During the Depression years they had to fix everything themselves, which meant he was never more in his element than when surrounded by screws and clamps and rivets and pins. As a kid, I'd tag along sometimes while he asked the clerk at the store for a pair of double-eared joint flanges, or some such thing, and then, while he was under the car on a mechanic's creeper, he'd stick his hand out and call for the piece he needed, as if it were as normal as a Tootsie Roll. Then he'd wheel out and see me just sitting there, tongue-tied.

"What are ya?" he'd say. "Dumb?"

That was back in a time when people would talk about "dumb animals" or even folks who were "deaf and dumb." At first it just sounded insulting, but later I learned it referred to the inability to speak. In my case, I was pretty sure both meanings applied.

Of course, it's even worse in French. No matter how long you've studied a foreign language, it's always a blanket that's a bit too small. If you pull it up to your neck, your feet stick out. If you roll onto your side, your butt is exposed. It made me especially sympathetic to Anne, whose blanket of language was shrinking all the time. Worse, with her, it was English that was vanishing. With dementia, your mother tongue becomes foreign. You scramble to hide what you don't know. You bluff your way through conversations, covering missed words with a laugh, or swerving when necessary into a new topic.

I use all the same strategies—only in French.

My go-to technique is called Fake-It-and-Wait. It starts when someone spouts something that goes over my head. Immediately, I pretend that I understand, tenting my fingertips and saying things like, *tell me more about that.* The longer you keep them going, the better the chance the word or phrase will come up again in the merry-go-round of the conversation. Sometimes it takes a while, and I find myself crossing out possibilities one by one, like a game of Clue where you're zeroing in on who bludgeoned Mrs. Peacock in the library with the lead pipe. You keep this going as long as you can, then you make a calculated guess among the options that remain.

As in so many aspects of life, patience is a virtue when it comes to misunderstanding. There are no downsides to postponing your assessment of a situation.

Take, for example, the time I was at a conference in a city north of Paris. We'd just finished the last session of the day, and a svelte young colleague invited me to grab a bite of dinner. Why not? After all, we were all stuck here for another day. And everyone has to eat. But no sooner had I agreed to the outing than she covered her mouth with her fingertips. "Oops!" she squeaked in French, "I forgot my *serviette*!" And she dashed from the hotel lobby, leaving me to wonder exactly what was up.

It was an *egrudecouleau* moment.

Now, a *serviette* is a napkin, but it seemed unlikely that this woman—so adept and sophisticated in other ways—was unaware that every restaurant in the neighborhood would eagerly provide her with all the napkins she required. I wondered if she was some kind of *professional* diner—like those top-notch bowlers who show up at the alley with their own ball in a satchel. That seemed a bit of a stretch, though. If she brought her own napkin, wouldn't she also need her own knife and fork?

Then a darker thought rolled in. For *serviette* can also mean a bath towel.

Egads.

Here we were, two colleagues sitting in a hotel lobby after a long meeting with hours of forced camaraderie, chuckling at one another's jokes. Just where did she think this night was going to end? Did she believe there was a pool in this antique hotel? Or a Turkish bath? Maybe she had a hot tub in mind—if such things even exist in France. I felt my throat tighten to the point of wheezing. Was it possible she didn't know I was a married man? All the clichés about French eroticism formed a conga line in my imagination, and my stomach churned. I'd have to let her down easy. *It's not you*, I'd say, *it's me*.

I'd nearly worked out the whole script by the time she returned to the lobby with a briefcase in hand. She'd left it back in the meeting room.

Inexplicably, *serviette* doesn't just mean a piece of cloth for wiping or covering yourself, but also a small valise for carrying documents.

Yes, this was a case where giving it a little time worked to my advantage.

Anne had wanted a book for finding words, but dictionaries are of limited use. After all, they define words with other words, and you barely emerge from one rabbit hole before falling into another. Worse yet, the list of definitions can be as long as your sleeve. You hear the word *bark*, but how do you know if they're talking about trees or dogs?

When does *racket* refer to noise instead of tennis? How do you choose?

French is even worse on the definition front. The language is filled with slippery fish. Take the word *hôte*, for instance, which means both host and guest. Or else *vert*, *vers*, *verre*, *vair*, and *ver*—words that sound exactly the same but have entirely different meanings.

These are all situations where time can be your friend.

I wish I could say that my linguistic challenges are limited to life in France, but I am often struck dumb in everyday conversation in the States, too.

Not long ago I make the mistake of asking a woman what she did, and she answered with a jumble that sounded like "Integrated marketing communications." I nearly said *Gesundheit* and offered a tissue, but instead trotted out the Fake-It-and-Wait technique. As she spoke, I crossed out options on my mental Clue card, but was still far away from figuring out whodunit. The elves that live inside my skull scrambled to build gingerbread models of what *integrated marketing communications* might be. A shopping mall, perhaps—one where the stores were connected to one another, joined by hallways. Or a socially progressive advertising campaign. Or a system where they start by selling you one thing, and then link the purchases until you're sitting on such a long line of overdue bills that you're afraid to stop, so you keep buying till the end of time.

All of which led me to another discovery: *Sometimes your native tongue can be as strange as a foreign language.*

We all struggle to stay afloat in the sea of words. It's just a question of degree. In fact, it might be that communication never worked the way we think it does. Maybe *egrudecouleau* isn't the exception, but the rule. We pretend to understand what our spouse or brother or boss has said—and because we sort of get the gist of it, or figure that we're about to, we pretend to understand it. And after a while, faking starts to feel like the real thing.

As Anne's disease progressed, she needed me to explain meal choices whenever we went to a restaurant. If you take into account all the regional sauces, the oddball vegetables and mystery spices, a French menu is harder to understand than symbolist poetry, or even Ikea instructions. I usually got the big picture, but when pressed for details, I'd be stumped.

"Fish," I'd say, translating the word she just pointed to. When her finger jumped to a different line, I'd offer up another helpful explanation: "More fish." I'm sure the dictionary would have told me it was cod or haddock or sea bream or fish sticks, but all I knew was that these were animals that swam in water. To me, they all blur together. It's like when you say "squirrel" a hundred times, and the word starts floating away from what you thought it meant.

How long do you give the meanings to settle? That is, when should you ask what the hell an *egrudecouleau* really is, and how long should you just roll with it?

A cousin of mine once told me a story about my dad that had been handed down in the family. It had to do with his relationship with his own father. Grampa Carpenter—a second generation German immigrant—was in his forties when my dad, Dean, was born, and by the time Dad was old enough to do much with him, Grandpa had reached the half-century mark, separating him from his own child by two generations. The old guy was standoffish and awkward. On the rare occasions they did things together, Grandpa refused to call his son by his real name. Instead, "Dean" became "Stu" in Grandpa's lingo. And since there were no Stewarts in the family, and Grandpa was famously fault-finding, Dad used the Fake-It-and-Wait technique until he figured it out. The nickname had to be short for Stupid.

On it went. Over the years, the old man would teach his son how to bait a hook or swing an ax, and as if dealing with a dolt, he'd say, "See, Stu? You do it like this." He'd show him how to use a clutch, and even when Dad mastered the actions instantly, the same question rang in his ears: "See, Stu?" Later on, Dad went off to the army, started a family. He earned a college degree. He climbed the corporate ladder. But nothing was good enough to please the patriarch. Stupid, Stupid, Stupid. The humiliations rained down.

What had he done to deserve a lifetime of put-downs?

It wasn't till he was in his thirties—when his own family was well established—that Dad confronted the old man, then in his seventies, soon to die of a heart attack.

They were out fishing. Grandpa was chattier than usual, unfurling one opinion after another. "See, Stu?" he said. "See, Stu?"

Finally Dad slammed down his rod. "Why?" he cried. "What did I ever do? Why is nothing ever good enough?"

"What on earth are you talking about?" the old man said.

Dad let him have it. The lifetime of rage boiled over. He railed against the nickname.

Grandpa's jaw dropped. No, he'd *never* called his son stupid. Not once. He loved the kid—clumsily perhaps, but in his own way. It wasn't "See, Stu," he'd been saying, but "*Siehst du?*" In the German of his youth, he was saying, Do you see? Do you get it? It was a special little phrase he used only with his youngest son, like a shared secret—that only one of them understood.

Fake-It-and-Wait? Maybe he should have asked sooner.

I did uncover an *egrudecouleau* at the Bricorama, but after I installed it, the toilet still leaked. What can I say? Sometimes the problem isn't language. It's just your plumbing skills that suck.

I also found the dictionary Anne was looking for. But she never used it. She still liked to read, but the words on the page didn't matter so much. After an hour or two, she'd put her book down, and later on I'd see that she'd never turned a page. Sometimes it's comforting just to sit with language. It's like hanging out with old friends, the kind where you never have to say much of anything.

And yet, there were times with Anne when language bubbled up unexpectedly.

One night we watched a campaign speech on TV.

"Ladies and gentlemen," Joe Biden cried, "I'm going to go all over this country, every part of the Democratic Party and be united—men, women; gay, straight; black, brown—"

He was hitting all the demographics.

Anne turned to me on the sofa. "What about the cats?" she said.

That took me aback. But you have to admit, she had a point. The Democrats had always talked a good game, promising a big tent, but who was looking out for the pets?

To be honest, after watching the presidential campaign, I wasn't so concerned about the cats and the dogs and the hamsters. They were likely to fend for themselves. No, the animals I really felt sorry for were the political ones, which is to say, that one class of animals that we can truly classify as dumb, but definitely not mute, because they always have more to say.

5

A Thing I Saw:
Escape Velocity

WOODEN POSTS ROSE FROM A SEA OF MULCH, connected by bars and netting, one of those vast contraptions for climbing and bouncing and rocking and twirling—actions that give such pleasure to small bodies, and indigestion to larger ones.

Two kids—maybe five years old—rocked forward and back on spring-loaded animals, a frog and rabbit. Another scaled a web of rope toward the top of a platform, maybe five feet above the ground. A child chased a balloon. A few others played tag, dashing about the playground, learning the rudiments of catching and being caught—crucial lessons for life.

Around this scene, parents sat on benches, chatting or scrolling on their phones. A grandma basked in a wedge of sunlight, her chin high, eyes closed.

Next to the playground ran an asphalt path that rose toward the main hill of the park, at the top of which a mother appeared with a small child, six or seven years old. He was a scrawny kid, barely as tall as his mother's hip, dressed in blue shorts and a polo shirt. At his side he walked a small bicycle.

The decline of the hill offered an advantage to novices, and in short order the boy had mounted his steed. The mother steadied him as he set into motion. Then he pulled away, wavering at first, but soon straightening. The bare knees pumped hard as he picked up speed, the grim face relaxing into a smile. Halfway down the hill, he'd reached escape velocity, faster than his mother could trot.

Freedom!

Unfortunately, another half of the hill remained, and that's when physics took over. The pumping knees could no longer keep up. The feet splayed from the pedals. The boy's smile turned tight, panicked. The bicycle wiggled. Then, just as he reached the flat, hurtling toward the playground, down he went, hard, in a pint-sized version of one of those Tour-de-France wipeouts, wheels and limbs sliding several feet on the asphalt before the whole mass shuddered to a stop.

Now was the time for high drama—for tears and yelps, for adults to rush over, for the reckless mother to come, finally, to the rescue, to kiss the skinned knee, to cradle the poor victim, to hug him to her heart.

But no grownups moved. The basking grandma still sunned herself. The mother continued her unhurried descent. And after collecting his wits, the boy rose to his feet. Wincing, he checked his scraped knee, giving it a rub.

Then he righted his vehicle and climbed back on, ready for another go.

Back in the US, Anne and I used to scurry over to kiss our kid's bruises and nurse their hurts. But on this side of the Atlantic, they teach the young ones to take their lumps.

6

'Tis the Season

OUTSIDE THE DISCOUNT SHOP in the rue de Rennes, a set of cut-rate wineglasses caught my eye. Like everyone else in Paris, I'm always on the lookout for that most elusive of unicorns: stemware that screams elegance while whispering affordability. This store is one of those shoebox-sized places that spill out onto a sidewalk, and it's a popular destination for cheapskates like myself. Shoppers from the neighborhood milled about, turning Quimper salt shakers in their hands, checking the heft of cutlery. There was a chill to the air. The shopkeeper wore wool gloves with the fingers cut off so he could operate the register. Because of the season, a counter was layered with wrapping paper.

A middle-aged woman in a tweed overcoat approached the checkout and placed a dish with scalloped edges by the register.

"I'll take this, please," she said in a small voice.

"I bet you will!" the shopkeeper snapped.

The gruffness seemed uncalled-for, and out of keeping with the fake garlands of spruce that conferred holiday cheer on the establishment. I wasn't the only one who turned to watch.

"I'm sorry…?" the woman murmured.

"What about the other one?" he barked.

There was a pause.

"The other *what?*"

"The one in your handbag."

The woman flushed red. She fumbled for words. I exchanged looks with the other bystanders.

"Maybe you should take that out, too," he said. "And pay for it."

"I don't know what you…"

"Oh, don't give me that! You want me to get the video?" He gestured at a small camera mounted on the ceiling. It was the same kind I'd recently recommended for our building when mystery turds were appearing in the *local poubelles*. My suggestion back then had been deemed scandalous, whereas here it counted as business as usual. Go figure.

"Shall I get it?" the shopkeeper pressed. "Then we can rewind and watch how you came through earlier this morning." He leaned in. "When you stole the first one."

Whoa. I wasn't expecting that.

I awaited the woman's protestations, her indignation. But none came. Instead, shrinking into her overcoat as though all eyes leveled upon her were firing X-rays, she rummaged for her billfold, threw a twenty-euro note on the counter, and scuttled away under bellowed admonitions never to return.

What, I wondered, had I just witnessed? Clearly this well-dressed woman had the means to pay, so her drive to shoplift came from elsewhere. Having already stolen one, she was now completing the set. Possibly she'd taken it on as a challenge. Or it sprang from some compulsion. Or maybe she was just like the rest of us, keen to get a good deal, or even the best deal there is—*something for nothing at all.*

Which is, when you think about it, what this season is all about. There's no greater pleasure than receiving something out of the blue, with nothing expected in return. And, come to think of it, that's what we had just received at the dis-count store—a bit of free drama, a real-life story performed gratis. I had half a mind to send a thank-you note.

I suppose I hungered for drama out on the streets because there were fewer and fewer scenes worthy of this term at home. That's not to say that losing a loved one to Alzheimer's is devoid of high emotion. Far from it. But that churn is internal and often invisible. Once you've fin-ished the shopping and cooking and cleaning and tending and supporting, you're left with a kind vacuum. I know I should speak of the moments of tenderness and quiet, or the mute communion of souls that accompany terminal illnesses. But the fact is, we had passed the point where communion occurred—at least on most days. When I regaled Anne with the tale of the shoplifter—a scene she would have relished in the past—she replied, "Oh." That was the whole commentary.

It left me with a sense of loss. Both Anne and I were being robbed. Someone had come through our life and cleared us out.

There are two words for the act of getting something for free. One is *gift*, the other *theft*. Each has to do with an unsolicited exchange of goods, and the intimate link between these two is incarnated by the holiday cat burglar who goes by the name of Santa. The way he slips into people's homes at night is beyond creepy, but because he doesn't take anything—and, in fact, usually leaves behind a bunch of stuff that no one really needs—he's excused from doing a perp walk at the police station, and is instead granted the status of a folk-hero. But make no mistake, the one-sidedness of the exchange makes people uneasy.

People wave away the Santa example on account of his not being real, but I've tested the principle myself. Back in high school, also around Christmas time, I smuggled a two-foot-long icicle into a Minnesota grocery store, stashing it in the frozen food aisle. There I peeled a price tag off a Swanson dinner and applied it to my lightning bolt of ice, which I then carried to the checkout, along with a package of cookies and an orange. The gum-chewing cashier rang up the first two items without flinching, but when she came to the icicle, her hand halted in midair. Her eyes widened.

"But that's an icicle," she said. She looked at me for a reaction. "We don't sell icicles." Then self-doubt struck a blow. "Do we?"

I stood my ground as she conferred with the cashier at the next register. Eventually a manager came over. The end result was that I left the store with a legally purchased icicle, and I'd provided a small event in the lives of several individuals. I don't mean to say that I was Santa Claus, but still.

Who knows? Maybe that cashier is still alive today, and late at night in the nursing home, a memory ripples through her clouded mind, and her dry lips silently mouth the words, *What the fuck?*

If that's not the Christmas spirit, I don't know what is.

There's nothing more suspicious than a person offering you something for free, and that's doubly true in Paris, which specializes in getting you to pay for things. That's why it feels so odd during the holidays. The trademark profiteering appears to recede. The city turns eerily placid, and you let your guard down. At a Christmas market you sip a cup of mulled wine, your tummy going warm in a sleepy way, and an hour later, when you wake from this holiday trance, you find yourself in front of a display window of dancing marionettes at the Galeries Lafayette. In your hand is a sack full of gifts from expensive stores. Your wallet is lighter.

What just happened? You were swindled by Paris.

It's the same thing when you walk down the street and hear the clink of metal behind you. A voice calls out, and you turn to find a young woman running up, holding out a gold ring that she says you dropped. Of course, it's not yours, and the two of you discuss whose it must be, and what to do about it, until—*quel miracle!*—she tells you to take it. It will be perfect for you to offer to your wife or lover, or maybe your dog. Only after you accept this gold-painted washer from a hardware store does she ask you for a small reward for finding the ring you never lost.

Christmas is the prime season for scams, known around here as *arnaques*. Because it's the season for giving, plenty of people are eager to take. At the entrance to the Metro station near my apartment, you often see young people in colored vests standing about with clipboards. They seek to sign you up for the newsletter of charitable organizations that don't exist but still need a sizeable donation. My favorite of these is the Regional Association for Handicapped Children Deaf and Dumb and Poor. (Their sign-up sheet provides this translation of their name as a courtesy for foreigners.) Despite having ticked all the boxes of neediness, the RAHCDDP is not a registered non-profit. It instead plays on the guilt you feel for not personally needing their services—that is, for being more or less able-bodied, not hard of hearing (merely inattentive), loquacious, and burdened with extra money.

There's another little con that takes place in trains, especially on the light rail to the airport. A tight-lipped person in a heavy overcoat trundles through the car, handing out a small card to each passenger—or, if the passenger declines the offer, placing this card on the seat next to them. The text explains that the person is deaf, and it makes an impassioned (though poorly spelled) appeal for assistance in the form of cash. One has to admire the ingenuity of the choice of this particular disability, which precludes any possibility of discussion with the individual. It is also more equitable, opening up the opportunity for scammers whose native tongue is not French. A few minutes after dropping off the card, the entrepreneur comes back through, harvesting donations from a few of the passengers—the ones who quite urgently need an organization of their own, something like the Regional Association for the Gullible and Naïve.

Personally, I'm not even against scams. I just want them to be worth the money. For my five or ten euros, I think I have a right to be properly hoodwinked. Many of these ploys are plodding and obvious. But if someone can play me like a fish and reel me in, haven't we both benefited?

My favorite is when you're never even sure it's a con, even after they fleece you. Back when I got my first job in Paris, I inherited the task of passing a bribe to a man who performed unnamed and unknowable services for our organization—making vague connections, lubricating relationships. *Fifi* was the name he went by. Once a year—usually around Christmas time—I was to treat this jovial flimflam man to lunch at a restaurant of his choosing. For the next two hours, he would regale me with tales of his past, present, and future. At the end of the meal, between the cheese course and the dessert, there would be a lull in the conversation. Fifi's eyes would brighten, and he would play the fingertips of one hand against the fingertips of the other. Jostled from my stupor, I would then glide the envelope across the table and murmur a thank you—not just from me, but on behalf of all those whom our friendly swindler had mysteriously assisted.

Gift or theft? I never figured it out. But the something-for-nothingness of it felt like Christmas.

And then an event turned all my assumptions upside down.

Not long ago, while plodding through Paris in search of presents, I happened upon a sad little shop with a sparse selection of gifts and even sparser customers, the last of whom exited just as I entered. The owner stood blankly at the register, a petrified scowl on her face. Almost certainly her mental abacus was assessing the sales from this crucial season, which had been depressed by the joint scourges of the economy and the plague, and she found her annual total wanting.

I was about to leave when I discovered a collection of fist-sized river stones with ponderous words engraved on their surface—things like *amour*, *merci*, and *patience*. I needed something for my sister-in-law, who helped so much with Anne whenever we were in the States. Kate was now retiring from her career as an administrator, so I opted for a stone bearing the word *liberté*—which is not just one of the three parts of the French national motto, but also what one most yearns for after a career in bureaucracy.

Still, even liberty has a cost, so I took my find to the stern matron at the register, who sighed and began ringing me up. But then her fingers froze on the keys. Her gaze had lit upon a blue and white debit card lying on the counter, evidently forgotten by the previous shopper, the one who'd left as I entered.

The prospect of something theatrical bloomed. At the very least I'd be treated to a rant about idiot customers. Maybe she'd whip out a pair of shears and snip this person's credit into confetti. Or, if I was very lucky, I'd watch her palm the card discreetly, in preparation for a vast campaign of identity theft.

Instead, she dashed out the door, scanned the crowd, and reunited the card with its owner. When she returned, I barely recognized her. It took me a moment to realize why. She'd been disfigured by a smile.

Holiday lights in Paris are mostly just beacons drawing you to the larger department stores. The skating rink in front of City Hall feels like a cheap imitation of Rockefeller Center. The grandeur of Paris smacks of commerce, but in a small and humble way the city manages to conjure up a seasonal sensation.

In my neighborhood we have our share of panhandlers, some of whom are also homeless. The sight of these people, most of them men, always stirs my sympathy. They are a constant reminder of the inequities and difficulties of life.

The most intrepid of these characters is an old amputee who typically parks his wheelchair outside the bakery, facing the door. Thus, as you exit with pastries that you'll soon share festively with friends, you confront this embodiment of the human condition. It's always a stark reckoning—one that prompts me to part with spare change.

But as the holidays reach their crescendo, our bakery *clochard* dons a Santa Claus jacket for his afternoon shifts, along with a red and white hat topped with a furry ball. Last time, after my donation, he smiled toothlessly and wished me a Merry Christmas. We chatted. The tone was so jovial, even *fraternal*, that I forgot to feel guilty about my own good fortune.

As a kid, it took me a while to realize that Christmas is a lie. I don't mean the Santa Claus part, which I never really believed in, because, well, just think about it. But the winter holiday promises Big while delivering Small. You're supposed to be able to put whatever you want on your wish list, but when I was five or six, my most ardent desire was to be seven or eight. I also wanted to be an astronaut. For three years running, I asked for a color TV for my room—and this was at a time when even the giant RCA where we watched classics like *Gilligan's Island* and *Bonanza* was black-and-white. None of those wishes were going to be granted, and after a while you realize that you should only aim for what's possible. That's when you resign yourself. You cross out "Apollo Saturn V rocket (real)" and write in "Legos."

What I really wanted for Christmas this year was a wife who hadn't lost herself, and maybe the return of all those friends who have died over the years. Instead, I asked for socks. That seemed to be within the range of the possible. You don't want to dwell on things, or else the self-pity party gets revved up, and you start wondering if it's all pointless—which, of course, it is, since we all know full well that one day the sun will explode, the universe will contract to the head of a pin, and the next Big Bang will obliterate even the memory of our existence. Best not to think about it, and just pretend that we matter.

Taking Anne out for a walk along the rue Bobillot, I watched families on the sidewalk. They were often holding hands, usually chatting. Some were stopping at florist shops, which do a sideline in Christmas trees at this time of year. Moms and dads were assessing the spruces and pines—known during this season as a *sapin de Noël.* A French Christmas tree comes with none of the baggage of its American cousins. When I was a kid, during that brief period in the history of our nation when *men were men*, the patriarch's job was to plant the family's fir or spruce in a metal stand, clamping it in place with the kind of bolts used to snug Frankenstein's neck. Because the hardware has been rusting since the previous Christmas, the job always called for lubricants, pliers, and vast amounts of choice language. The tree was sometimes injured in the process, and it usually tipped like that tower in Pisa. The officiant for this ceremony was originally my dad, though when Anne and I accrued a family of our own, I cast myself in the role of the martyr for this particular event.

In France, however, the chance for martyrdom is zilch. Christmas trees are sold pre-erected—planted in a split log, where they stand perfectly straight. You shell out fifty euros, drag it home, and plop it in your living room. The process takes five minutes and is entirely lacking in profanity. Where, I'd like to know, is the fun in that?

More than anything, I long for spectacle and surprise— qualities Paris usually offers in abundance, and for free. But this year, what was there to do? We didn't need a tree, especially since we'd be back in the States by the time of the big event. There were no stockings to stuff, and I didn't even have a Christmas dinner to prepare. We were really just waiting for something—anything—to happen.

I gave up hoping for drama, resigning myself to the perfunctory task of purchasing gifts for the kids, which we could bring back with us. This I did at a local department store, and as my bags grew heavier, so did my feet. At every stop the saleswoman wore me down with politeness. Around me was nothing but the buzz of voices, along with laughter, and even, as I exited the store, an odd and birdlike chirping.

At that moment someone latched onto my elbow. I turned to find a block-shouldered man in an ill-fitting blue suit standing beside me. The word *sécurité* was embroidered on his pocket, but I found his severe demeanor far from comforting.

"You'll want to come with me, Sir."

"I'm sorry? What's this about?"

He gave me a meaningful look. "We'll talk about that inside."

That's when I realized that the chirping hadn't been birds after all. I'd triggered the alarm. My bag had set things off. Probably one of the salesclerks had forgotten to remove a metal tag. Something hadn't been properly swiped.

"109?" the security man was saying into his sleeve. "This is 110. This is 110. We have a blue."

Another thought blossomed. Maybe, *just maybe,* this was the beginning. The first scene. Perhaps one of the clerks had added another article to my bag—one I hadn't purchased, that couldn't be explained away, rather like that icicle so many years ago. The police would become involved. I'd get to visit the *commissariat.* Who knows? Perhaps I'd get to spend Christmas in a French jail.

The grip on my elbow tightened, and my companion yanked me forward. We were headed for an office, an interrogation.

Deep down, I knew it wouldn't last. I had a receipt for every article in the bag. But for now, my lungs swelled. The air was fresh, the fluorescent lights sparkled. Paris was back!

Isn't the greatest gift of all a surprise—the introduction of an instant of doubt when everything is possible, both fortune and failure, where your life twists at the end of a thread?

That's what I got this year. A little present, just for me. Turns out, there really is a Santa Claus after all.

7

Grand Finale

AT LONG LAST WE PLOPPED into our seats in row 32, Anne's
sister at the window while I manned the aisle, our charge
wedged between us so we could attend to her needs. The
morning had been rough, Anne unpacking her suitcase
faster than I could fill it, the cats so thoroughly underfoot
that she nearly fell, the question coming every five minutes
about where we were going, and my reply — *Paris…Paris…
Paris…* — which each time she found pleasantly surprising, especially the part about traveling with Kate, her artsy
sister with the winning smile. At airport security her full
pockets triggered the metal detector, leading to a pat-down
she tried to swat away. For a while her purse went missing.
There was a complicated bathroom break. During boarding,
she wanted her sweater on, then off, then on again. By the
time we reached the seats, Kate and I were already ragged. I
craned my neck. Any chance that drink cart might make an
early appearance? But no, the cabin doors were closing. The
jetway pulled back, and we rolled into motion.

"I want to get up," Anne said.

I whispered that she couldn't.

Kate patted her arm. "Not right now, Nubba," she said, trotting out the childhood nickname.

"I want to get up," she declared. "I want to get up!"

I exchanged a look with my sister-in-law. The eyes said it all. We were just beginning to fathom what a colossal mistake we'd made.

One last time. That was the plan. Anne and I had been coming to Paris almost every year since we married, scores of trips, with kids and cats and careers in tow, so how could we let it all go, just like that?

It was nobody's fault—well, except maybe 100% Kate's. *Shouldn't we take her?* she said. *One last time?* The answer was glaringly obvious: nope, we shouldn't, absolutely not, forget it, out of the question. *Non.*

"Sure," I replied. "Why not?"

And then, before I knew it, we were there, on the plane. For the next eight hours, Anne barely closed her eyes, despite sleeping ten hours a night at home. There was a spilled drink, the constant changing of channels on the screen, the Incident of the Lost Ear Buds, all topped by the flight attendant having to bust into the bathroom to get her out. When we arrived in the apartment on the rue Bobillot, I guided her to the bedroom, where she promptly conked out, her head at the foot of the bed. In the living room, Kate had collapsed on the couch, bleary-eyed, thumbing words into her phone.

"Talking to Bill," she said, referring to her husband. "Having him check flights to see if we can turn around and head straight back."

We were both wondering the same thing—namely, if we'd survive this trip.

Anne had been declining for the better part of a decade, but now she was also physically unsure of herself. I'd learned that the hard way, a year earlier when we visited Jacques and Pascale in the Alps. Although in his seventies, Jacques still likes to leap into the void every now and then, opening his wings for a bit of paragliding. Pascale prefers to have her feet on the ground. One day we trekked up to a restaurant near a summit. Anne managed it. But mountain trails are like opera singing—it's harder to go down than up. She struggled with the thousand small thoughts it takes in order to walk on an uneven path. After her second tumble, I piggybacked her the rest of the way down, till we found a village.

At the pharmacy they wrapped her ankle.

"Oh my," Anne repeated. "I'm so sorry. I'm so sorry." She was embarrassed to have caused such a stir.

"What's she saying?" the pharmacist asked me in French.

"Thank you," I said. "She's saying thank you."

Because her language was fading, too.

Anne had learned "high-school French," which is a dialect spoken in no country in the world. She took one course in college. And a few years later she dredged it all up on account of me, chipping away at the grammar and vocabulary, year after year, and then watching our son and daughter pass her up and leave her behind in the linguistic dust. Still, she'd become capable, was able to converse, stopped freaking out about the grammar.

And then, bit by bit, it started crumbling away, tiles falling from the mosaic. French disappeared fast. In the right circumstances I could still draw greetings from her, but that was it.

Soon, though, it was English that posed a problem. Spelling had never been Anne's strong suit, but now it turned phonetic, and then almost random. Words eluded her. Sentences trailed off. After dinner each night, I'd sit with her on the couch while she nursed a glass of wine, and we engaged in conversations that I only half-understood. For her, our house in Minnesota had become her childhood home. A neighbor named Lucy merged with an old school friend of the same name. There were nights I barely knew in what universe she was living. I strained to understand, to connect the words. How could it be so hard?

Then I got it. English had become the new French. Her native tongue had turned into a foreign language. She had to think before she spoke. She tried to force the pieces together, even when they didn't fit, the way I do jigsaws.

"Uh-huh," I'd tell her. "I see."

Though usually I didn't see. I was just like one of those French waiters who smile through gritted teeth while trying to figure out what the hell the American in front of him has just uttered. *An excellent choice, Monsieur*, they say, hoping the customer won't notice when they're served something entirely different.

And Anne never did.

If you're losing your memory, Paris isn't a bad place to end up, for the city specializes in the unforgettable. You'd have to be pretty far gone not to recognize the Arc de Triomphe or the Eiffel Tower, and even if the names of these places linger stubbornly on the tip of your tongue, refusing to jump off, you'll probably know you've been there before, even if you haven't. After all, the whole purpose of monuments is to commit things to memory.

The thirteenth arrondissement isn't blessed with giant obelisks or glitzy opera houses, but it holds plenty of modest shrines to personal pasts. *There*, I find myself thinking, is the florist's shop where we got the Christmas tree that year. *Over there* is where I watched firemen pull a woman from a third-story window and carry her down the ladder. And *there* is the gate in the park where our son nearly crushed his finger in first grade.

Fancier parts of the city are pocked with bronze plaques telling you not to forget that Victor Hugo lived at such-and-such an address, or that Marie Antoinette was imprisoned here before they lopped her head off. But if my neighborhood had plaques, they'd say things like, *Here lived Pauline and Jacques Dupont, rather happily, for thirty years*, or *Here a woman named Marie-Louise played the piano every afternoon at four*, or *In this building a fat man died and it took four people to carry him down the stairway*. Small memories, but important ones.

In Anne's case, she still recognized certain sights in our neighborhood. The bakery was familiar. So was the Parc Montsouris, that great green space of the south side, right where the thirteenth meets the fourteenth. There, past the trees, she loved to watch the black swans in the pond, along with the water hens, the turtles, and the enormous carp who sometimes breached the surface. But somehow these destinations were no longer anchored on her internal map. She had no idea if they were near or far, if you could get there on foot, or if it required overnight travel. And because she no longer knew where to go, she followed the same directions always, turning to the right every time she stepped out a door or came to a corner. I never let her walk by herself, of course, but if I had, I think she'd have been fine, making endless loops around our city block, like a lone car in a NASCAR race—one that goes in excruciatingly slow motion.

The old joke about the good side of Alzheimer's is that you're always meeting somebody new. In Anne's case, she was also crossing paths with old acquaintances she'd never met. We ran an errand to a housewares store in the center of town, and on the way, she pointed out a woman with a deep blue scarf, and then a man with a little terrier on a leash. Each time, she commented on how she knew these anonymous passersby. She'd seen them before. And when we got to the shop, she remembered it, despite never having been there.

Kate took Anne on pilgrimages to places where we'd lived before we bought the apartment. They spent time in cafés. One day we hiked out to the Bois de Vincennes on the eastern edge of the city, and I rowed us around the artificial lake, just as we'd done with the kids, years ago. There's nowhere to go on that stretch of water, so I propelled us in circles, reproducing in miniature the pointlessness of the entire voyage.

What exactly *were* we doing here? Why *had* we come back to Paris?

Kate and I talked about it. It was to make Anne happy, we told one another. We'd made some kind of noble sacrifice. The more we talked, the more insistent we became, and the more insistent we became, the less we actually believed it, and the less we believed it, the more desperate the conversation grew. In the end, the gold finish had rubbed off the pretty idea we'd started with, leaving us with a knob of clay.

Fact was, we'd tricked ourselves into thinking the trip was for her. That helped us avoid seeing we were doing it for ourselves. The two of us suffered from the same delusion—namely, that there was still some *there* there in Anne's head. This was the secret that was so secret we hadn't even shared it with each other. Instead, we'd allowed ourselves to half-think there'd be something curative about the return, as though Anne would see Notre-Dame Cathedral and experience a jolt of recognition, all our previous visits flickering across the screen of her memory. The idea was to connect the dots, location by location. We'd emerge from the Metro Station at Jussieu, and the apartment we'd rented years ago—the attic one that looked like an overturned ship's hull—would leap to mind. We'd turn a corner, and the view of the Roman arena where the kids used to play would trigger a gust of exhilaration. The past would reconnect to the present, and all would be well.

Or not.

Instead, things slid from bad to worse. As though to punish me for writing about public toilets, plumbing problems, human turds in the *local poubelles*, and dog shit on the stairs, bathrooms became Fate's way of wagging her bony finger at me. Anne went to powder her nose in a restaurant and never returned, requiring an emergency intervention. Day after day, Kate's presence proved indispensable, thanks to the natural inclination of females of the species to pee collectively. One night, Anne got up from bed to use the toilet, couldn't find the right door, and humiliation ensued.

"What do you think?" I asked Kate the next morning. "We could fly standby."

It was August. The planes were packed. If we managed to get seats at all, they'd be scattered throughout the cabin. That prospect flashed bleakly entertaining scenes through my mind: Anne chatting with neighbors who didn't understand English, or the flight attendant taking her meal choice, or that sweater going on and off every five minutes—all while Kate and I sawed logs in Comfort Plus. But no, surely there was a law against such a thing.

Would we make it? There was still another week to go.

Kate hit upon the idea of art. She set up a miniature studio at the dining room table, where she worked from photographs of the park to create watercolor versions of the same scenes. Anne joined in. One photo showed a dramatic view of the pond, with willows weeping at the water's edge, the great green hill rising in the background, a rocky outcropping where a stream trickled down. It was all shades of green and blue, puffs of white overhead.

Anne's version was black. She'd put all the colors together, and swirled a vortex with the brush, creating the mouth of a cave, or a portal to the next dimension. Some of it continued on the tablecloth.

"That's great," I told her. And it sort of was, but mostly because she'd successfully painted what her life was like on the inside.

It was around then that Kate and I began to lose our own minds. I'd go to the market and come back with only half of what we needed, not even able to locate my list. Kate got turned around on an excursion with Anne, and had no idea how to get back. Was today Monday or Friday? When I asked Kate, she had no idea either. I left a pot on the stove too long. Kate pulled clean laundry from the dryer, only to deposit it straight back into the washing machine.

We each tried to ignore our own rapid decline, but one night, after Anne went to bed, we confessed our anxieties to one another—the fear that it was catching! Spending so much time with a demented person was making us more like her. Unless our utter exhaustion had something to do with it. After all, we were constantly on high alert, monitoring the door, checking her whereabouts, helping with her clothes, her food, her bath, her glasses. Simply putting a cheery face on irrevocable disaster takes a colossal toll.

We reassured each other we weren't losing it—although the fact that the other person clearly *was* losing it made those assurances suspect.

Walking anywhere with Anne meant seeing the city through the eyes of someone who'd never seen it before, had barely heard of it. You appreciated all over again the many small surprises that come from turning a corner or cresting a hill. Not far from our building is a shop that specializes in locks. Their window display hasn't changed in twenty years, but suddenly Anne found it engrossing, and so, therefore, did I. Who knew there were so many ways to reinforce your front door, or to add three-point deadbolts? The keys alone were as ornate as Fabergé eggs. In the street, a piece of litter might draw her attention more than any architectural marvel, and at her side I found myself studying door handles, stains, and broken glass with the kind of scrutiny I usually reserved for paintings at the Musée d'Orsay.

It wasn't just the way I saw the city that changed. It was also how the city saw me—at least the people in it. I noticed this while helping her choose socks at a department store one day. Kate had told me she needed some simple white anklets, but Anne kept reaching for knee-highs with complicated patterns. As I gently policed her selection, the saleswoman's eyes burned through the back of my neck. *Oh yeah,* she was thinking, *he's one of those.* It was the same look I got in restaurants when I ordered for her. Here was another guy speaking for his wife, taking every choice out of her hands and controlling her life.

Worst of all, they were kind of right.

On the last day of our trip, we celebrated our imminent return with a blow-out dinner in a restaurant built in an ancient wine cellar. Anne enjoyed her favorite duck dish, which she experienced as a novelty. Kate and I raised our glasses. A couple toasts were made. It was celebratory but subdued—a going-away party for a very different kind of departure.

If we'd known ahead of time how this trip was going to go, we'd never have left home. But I suppose that's why

PARIS LOST AND FOUND

life is built the way it is, the future always feeling vague and unproblematic, a can that you can always kick farther down the road. You put life on a credit card because it'll be easier to pay in the future. You commit to misery tomorrow in exchange for a bit of fun today. That's how we're put together. It's in our DNA—the way you don't get a baby until long after the sex. When all the difficulties are nine months away, you just go for it.

Or is it just me?

Moreover, the dread of what's coming is often seasoned with hope. In two years, maybe you'll have enough money to pay that bill. Perhaps the chore you promised to do won't be so bad. And hey—maybe being a mom or a dad will be fun. Best of all, by the time you get there, no matter how bad it is, a new future will flicker dimly in the distance. And because everything looks better in low light, hope will creep back in.

That last night in Paris, I took Anne for a stroll through the neighborhood, stopping at all her favorite sights. She was somehow blissful. But in my mind, I was checking off the list. Here was the last time she'd see the bakery. The last time she'd cross this street. The last whiff of wisteria by the row houses. The last game of *pétanque* in the park. The last splashes from the swimming pool. The last view of our building. The last climb up our stairs. And, from our living room overlooking the little square, the last sunset in Paris—which is the best kind of sunset, thanks to the creamy glow of the limestone that gives this city its special hue.

"Has it been a good trip?" I asked her.

"Oh yes," she said.

"We leave in the morning, you know."

"Do we?" She pulled her sweater tight as she peered out the window. "I can't wait for next time."

8

Lockdown

AND THEN, AS IF THAT WEREN'T BAD ENOUGH, a few months after our return to the States, people started getting the sniffles. Two days later their throat itched, which led to shortness of breath and soon a hacking cough. Faster than you could say *egrudecouleau,* folks were queueing up for a stint on a respirator—which sometimes wasn't enough. The illness had started in a petri dish in Wuhan, or maybe on the scales of a long-snouted animal called a pangolin, and just like that the world was shutting down, planes were grounded, hotels and restaurants shuttered. All of a sudden people had time to do those things they'd been putting off for years—but instead of learning to play the harmonica or building that toolshed, they poured their energies into decrying masks, or decrying the decriers of masks, or maybe just crying.

We fell into that last category. After the disastrous farewell tour in Paris, we'd remained homebound. Anne's decline had accelerated, her language vanishing as fast as her balance. A rag-tag army of friends and aides helped keep her active and safe, filling in during the times when I was teaching or shopping or cooking or cleaning, or while I stuck grip strips on the stairs or swapped out the stove for a locking version.

But like a house of cards, the support network only looked solid, and it flew apart when that viral breeze blew in. Suddenly no one was allowed to enter anyone else's home, and going outside wasn't a great option either. Just to pick up groceries, people dressed like astronauts or members of the Byrd Expedition.

The world was buttoning up, and in a rush our little family council made a decision. We found Anne a bed in a care home just days before all the facilities went into lockdown.

It was only after we settled her in her new accommodations, leaving her behind as we drove home, that a pressure valve inside of me opened up, and I realized how close I'd come to a major plumbing failure in the vicinity of my heart.

As luck would have it, Paul had caught the disease *du jour* in the deadly first wave in New York, and he had the antibodies to prove it. For a time, this made him the only family member allowed to visit Anne, while the rest of us eavesdropped with Zoom.

End Times are always bleak, but the pandemic added a rich layer of garnish to the shit sandwich we'd been served—all of us, that is, except Anne, who loved her new little home with its '60s-era Muzak and the artificial cat that purred mechanically in her lap. Even as she descended into an inner world of illusion, she remained the happy-go-lucky person I'd married—except for that blankness in the eyes.

Days became weeks, weeks became months. Anne went into hospice. And then out. The kids traveled back and forth when they could. And our old family home grew larger by the day. The house was haunted by all Anne's affairs in the dressers and closets, but when I gave the clothing away, the emptiness just increased the echo. In the end, I put the house on the market, packing and cleaning in Covid-induced solitude. The very last day, before handing over the keys to the new owners, I painted over the closet door where we'd recorded the kids' heights every year with a dark pencil.

I moved to a condo closer to the care home. And a few months later, Anne entered a stage of the disease known as *lingering*. That's when the person has left, but no one informed the body. In such a situation, the spouse has a lousy role. You come and go. You talk to the person. You hold her hand or brush her hair. You reminisce about the good and bad. There are moments of tenderness, but they're all one-sided. The Anne you knew has departed, leaving no forwarding address.

And that's where we'll draw the curtain on this little narrative. Not out of modesty or even pain, but simply because of the sheer monotony of the very long business of dying. The disease had erased Anne slowly for more than a decade, and there was still a bit of scrubbing to do before the slate of her existence would be wiped clean.

The kids and I kept up our visits at the same time we made our peace with where this was headed. It was time to catch our breath.

For me, that meant settling into my new home. There was still a pandemic to get through. And when you've been reduced to pretty much nothing, living by yourself after four decades of togetherness, it turns out there's still one question left: what now?

PART TWO

The Middle

Though tossed by the waves,
she will not sink.

— Motto of the City of Paris

9

Ghost Town

TWO YEARS PASSED, AND LIKE EVERYONE ELSE I was crushed under the heel of time. When finally borders reopened and I straggled back to Paris, my roller bag strangely heavy with loss, I craved normalcy, a whiff of something familiar. Our little family had been drained by Anne's illness and the pandemic. The kids were both on the East Coast, getting their own lives back into motion. As for me, what I craved more than anything was the bustle of the city, the vibrant life of a world capital—one where I had my bearings, my past, my friends, my apartment.

Instead, I found a ghost town—shops closed and boarded up, the population vanished. The only thing missing was tumbleweed.

Paris, too, had been put through the mill over the past couple of years. Like me, the city was struggling to recover.

My favorite restaurant had been a hole-in-the-wall affair with seating for twelve. A lone cook used to labor in the kitchen, juggling quail eggs and sauteing shellfish, while his colleague, a woman with long legs and a firecracker wit worked the tables. The food was above average, but it was mostly ambiance they sold, the camaraderie that comes from sitting elbow to elbow with your neighbors as wisecracks ricochet off the walls. And though I no longer had anyone to eat with, I trudged down the street to see the old gang.

Gone. *Fermé*. Closed for good.

In my bakery, I chatted with one of the saleswomen, the one with brown hair that she now dyed sandy blond. Her colleague, whom I'd known for twenty years, had fallen ill with the plague *du jour*, she told me, and after struggling through a long recovery had thrown up her hands and retired. I'd never see her again.

I consoled myself by ordering a croissant, and as I counted out my coins, the sandy hair swished as the woman wagged her head.

"What's the problem?" I asked.

"*Je prends la carte*," she said, meaning she wanted me to pay my 90 centimes with a bank card. That's when I learned that nobody used cash here anymore. Lucre was considered filthy, germ-ridden.

Nothing was the same. My building was half-empty. The outdoor market was threadbare, a shadow of its former self. The streets were so deserted that you could actually park.

And it wasn't just the tourists who'd gone missing. No, even Parisians had bailed on Paris. The height of the pandemic had included a lockdown, long stretches known as *le confinement*, when schools and daycares and cinemas were closed, when you couldn't go out after dark, or wander far from home, or walk your dog without a permission slip.

The order to stay at home was hard for everyone, but especially for those who didn't have a home to stay in. My neighborhood has its fair share of homeless—known here as *sans-domicile-fixe*, or SDFs, though to be honest some of them are only semi-homeless, sleeping in shelters that close their doors during the day. Before the pandemic, you'd find a cluster of SDFs hanging out on the steps of the church down the street, chatting, sipping on beers, asking passersby for a coin or two. *J'ai pas de monnaie*, people used to lie, claiming they were out of change, tired of being tapped for funds at every street corner.

But now, even the SDFs had flown the coop, mostly. On the church steps there were just a couple left. When they asked for a handout, people said the same thing as before—*j'ai pas de monnaie*—but this time they meant it, since coins and bills had vanished from everyday life. Covid had been hard on a lot of professions, and begging was one of them.

Parisians suffered during the lockdown. In this city, the average person makes do with 300 square feet of living space. Such dimensions are hard for Americans to imagine, especially if they're from the Midwest, living in suburban homes where they might go an entire day without catching sight of their children, the ones who live on some other floor of the same house, they think. By comparison, 300 square feet is pretty tight. It's bigger than a prison cell, but not by much, so people went a little stir-crazy.

Which is why my friends had jumped ship. Guy and Sabine—stalwart Parisians I'd known for three decades, whose kids had trick-or-treated with ours, back when Halloween made its debut in France, who marched in protests as a form of entertainment, and made paella in a giant saucer like the one I used to go sledding in as a kid, and above all, who *scoffed* at the provinces—they had cracked. Sabine snatched at early retirement. Guy tried to hang on, and then gave in. Now they were living in Perpignan on the Mediterranean.

Per-fucking-*pign-an!* I couldn't believe it.

I Zoomed with them. Either the lighting was odd or something had gone wrong with their skin, no longer pasty white. And what had become of the Parisian scowl?

"What's the matter?" I said. "You look different."

Sabine shrugged. "It's the sun."

"No, no," Guy countered. "The beach."

"Ok, so the sun *and* the beach."

"When are you coming back?" I sounded whiny, like a kid whose parents had moved away while he was out.

The longer they beat around the bush, the more my heart sank. They weren't coming back. Ever. Except the way visitors pass through the capital.

Then there was Thomas. He'd lived in the fourteenth arrondissement for as long as I'd known him. Perennial

renters, he and his husband had been looking to buy, maybe
in my neighborhood, maybe on the right bank. They'd been
scrutinizing the ads, visiting properties. Then Covid hit.
They hunkered down, took it as long as they could, but finally
headed for the hills. And not just *any* hills. No, they went to
the Pyrenees, and then crossed them, and kept going. They
were now living in Spain, coming to Paris only occasionally.

There's a famous French poem that talks about losing
the people you love. "A single soul goes missing," Lamartine
moans, "and the whole world is empty." But this wasn't just
one person I'd lost. There was Anne, of course. But now it
was also Guy and Sabine. Thomas. Even Jacques and Pascale
barely came through Paris anymore. And Catherine? She and
Philippe had set up shop in the southwest, where they had
enough room to swing a cat—maybe even several cats. Who
knows? I hadn't been able to visit them yet, because that
would have meant taking the train, and the train required a
Covid pass, and Covid passes were hard to come by.

Speaking of which.

In the States we all received vaccination cards handed
out by the pharmacies or the clinics, or simply forged on
someone's printer. It wasn't exactly high security. France, on
the other hand, pulled out all the stops. There's nothing the
French like more than the opportunity to set the steamroller
of public administration into motion. Each and every person got their vaccine status translated into a QR code, one
that granted you access to movie theaters and restaurants

and public transportation. That meant that every business needed to be able to scan your code, which, at first, most of them couldn't.

To make matters worse, they'd been in such a rush to roll things out that they overlooked a few details—like *me*. Americans were arriving with cards that were entirely legible to the human eye, but inscrutable to the electronic beams designed to read squares filled with other squares. Without the QR code you couldn't so much as enter a café to buy a coffee—much less the stiffer drink that most of us needed.

Rumors swirled about how to convert the American version into the French one. For a while people whispered that the consulate could pull off this magic, and the ensuing siege of the American Embassy reminded me of scenes of the US departure from Saigon. Then word got out that the vaccination centers—set up in gymnasiums throughout the city—were authorized to perform conversions. But that was just a diversionary tactic by the embassy, a trick to get us off their front lawn. Next it was the pharmacies. On various websites you'd hear that such-and-such a drugstore in the Marais was doing conversions, but as soon as 500 Americans lined up outside for this free service, they closed their doors. Rumors flew. There was perhaps a pharmacy in the seventh doing it—or else the twelfth, or the sixteenth. They opened and closed. Crowds swerved from one to the next.

Here in the thirteenth, I took it upon myself to canvass all the options. What does it say about the health of my neighbors that there are 11 pharmacies in easy walking distance? I went to each one, plying my charm.

"*Excusez-moi de vous déranger*," I said, ingratiating myself as best I could, "*mais j'ai un problème.*"

Usually this phrase turned the key on people's hearts. Saying you had a problem made people take pity on feckless Americans, and they would offer assistance the way you'd help anyone with a disability. But this time, no such luck. The white-coated woman or man before me could solve my aches and pains, but they had no idea how to turn me into a French person—that is, the kind of person who might have access to a QR code. My first stops met with blank stares. At the fourth pharmacy, the woman had heard of such a conversion, but had no idea how to perform it.

"Have you tried the embassy?" she said.

Onward I trekked. Again and again I excused myself for deranging them. The next one was a no, followed by another no, then a maybe-but-not-sure-how, and then another redirect to the embassy. It was at the second-to-last on my list that I found a harried woman who at first rebuffed my request, but paused, cocked her head. Maybe she *had* heard of this. Yes, her colleague had muttered something about it. He may even have left a note.

Customers were starting to bunch up behind me, eager to purchase their hair ointments and sanitary pads, but my middle-aged heroine puffed a lock of hair from her eyes and began pawing through her papers, rummaging at the counter.

Finally she uncovered a scrawled series of notes including all the magic words needed to accomplish the impossible through the national pharmacy database.

She fired up the ancient computer, logged on, began clicking uncertainly. Peering over the top of her glasses, she hunted and pecked, backspaced, pecked again, stopping to glance at the growing herd of customers awaiting her services.

When I offered to help, her face unpinched with relief, and while she began ringing folks up, I took over the command post that provided unfettered access to the pharmaceutical records of 65 million French citizens. Fifteen minutes later a dot-matrix printer was whining out my QR code.

Eureka.

I was now vested with the power to buy myself a cup of coffee, where I'd also have to pay with *la carte*. En route to the nearest café, a rare SDF appeared and asked for a handout. I patted my pockets, only to realize I was now like everyone else.

"*J'ai pas de monnaie*," I told him. The process by which large bills are broken into small ones, then eroded into silver coins, and finally into crumbs of jingling copper, was out of whack.

The fellow sighed. Life wasn't what it used to be.

All of Paris was odd, out of sorts. At the height of the pandemic, wildlife returned to the city. In the south there were rumors of boars trotting through towns. On the ring road circling

Paris, you'd find a mother duck leading ducklings across the lanes. Fox cubs were spotted in one of the cemeteries.

But the people had gone weird, too—at least the ones that hadn't pulled up stakes and lit out for the countryside. When I'd left the States, some kind of feud had been raging between the Hatfields and McCoys. One side felt that everyone should wear bandana-like coverings over their mouth and nose, whereas the other insisted that such a measure was degrading in the extreme. Nothing was more important than the bandana debate. Hurricanes rolled through, fires raged, but all you heard was people yelling back and forth. They had come to blows more than once. But the end result was that if you were a Hatfield you wore a bandana, while the McCoys did not, and this helped you identify who you wanted to pick off with your six-shooter. It was, to put it mildly, confusing.

Whereas in Paris they were all Hatfields! Everyone wore a bandana, and it didn't seem to bother them. Now and then you'd catch sight of someone who looked like a McCoy, but if a Hatfield offered this renegade a covering for his mouth and nose, he accepted it—and often said *merci* in the process. Even the homeless guys wore them, most of the time. Maybe that's what people gave when they didn't have any *monnaie*.

There was a downside to all the masking, though. It introduced space.

In France, people who are engaged in conversation stand closer together than their American counterparts. Yanks prefer a bit of breathing room between themselves and their fellow man, but if you're having a discussion with a French person, you may find yourself backing up as she keeps approaching. Six inches between your nose and theirs is not uncommon, and that's not even intimate. During Covid, though, the spaces widened. The rule of thumb became six feet—just far enough that your outstretched hands couldn't meet.

And this also made kissing difficult.

Let me explain.

Back when I was a teenager in the US, I spent a lot of time admiring the miracle of lip-contact, which existed only theoretically for me, since my encounters with young women triggered vaporizing looks of scorn. In France, however, which I began to frequent at the same age, I was not just *allowed* to kiss female creatures, but even *expected* to— just on their cheeks, to be fair, but twice, except in parts of Normandy or the south, where it was three or even four times. This was known as *la bise*.

Salutations with men were different, depending. Handshakes were the usual thing—a rather limp affair in the French version, as if the other person's mitt had turned into a trout that had died some time ago, and was left to soften in the sun.

When you showed up at a mixed gathering, you'd go round the entire table: kiss, trout, kiss, trout, trout, kiss. By the time you finished, it was nearly time to leave, which meant starting the cycle all over again.

One evening, when I was in my twenties, I arrived at a party and a friend approached. To my horror, he bore down as if to plant a wet one on my lips, veering off at the last instant to my cheek, the way a motorcyclist plays chicken with a brick wall. It was the *bise* once more, but performed by a man. I'd seen this in movies, but only when members of the Resistance left on missions of certain death. Here it meant I'd made it to the inner circle.

Being kissed by men toward whom you are not romantically inclined is unsettling at first, but like everything else, you get used to it.

The problem, of course, is getting un-used to all the kissing. During the Covid era the touchy-feely part of French greetings went into quarantine, but old habits were hard to break. You'd see masked people crossing paths on the sidewalk. They'd pause and squint, as though the eyes or haircut of the other person had something familiar about them. Then recognition would strike, and as they called out greetings, the two would lean in for *la bise*, jumping back at the last instant as they remembered they weren't supposed to do this anymore, rather like teenage lovers when a parent walks into the room.

As for me, now quite alone in Paris, I found myself hankering for contact. Not kisses, necessarily, but with so many friends having flown the coop, even a limp trout in the hand would have been welcome. However, by that point, even the shaking of hands had become *problématique*. For the first time ever, I saw French people giving one another fist-bumps—referred to, inexplicably, as *le check*.

Frankly, the most distressing thing was to watch first- and second-graders outside their school in the morning. In olden days they'd have been slobbering greetings all over one another. But with grownup masks on those tiny faces, your chance of even identifying a cheek wasn't great, much less landing on one. I didn't spot any six-year-olds giving each other *le check*, but it wouldn't be long. The end of civilization couldn't be far away.

Trying to conduct life in France without the *bise* or the handshake is a bit like conversing with an Italian whose arms are tied behind his back. You know something is broken. The big question was, was it broken for good?

People talked about this. Some thought the change was for the best, which is to say that not everyone had been crazy about getting kissed all the time by people they barely knew and maybe didn't even like. And the more I thought about it, the more the act of shaking hands seemed peculiar and otherworldly—the kind of thing aliens might do. Your fingers wrap around another person's palm, and then you pump up and down. Who came up with that?

There was speculation that kids might never learn the same habits of physical contact. The cycle had been interrupted. Getting rid of all that kissing and pawing was clearly a more hygienic way to live, but still, something was lost in the process—a little luxury called *touch*.

Paris has always had trouble with change. People flock to the city because of how well it wears the past. It's never been locked in amber, like a mosquito in *Jurassic Park*, but there is a kind of steadiness to the place. Thus, as the pandemic waned, a sort of normalcy returned. Bit by bit, the empty parking spots filled. The outdoor markets expanded their awnings and offerings. Even the *bise* made a return, and *le check* receded.

Still, it wasn't quite business as usual. Some folks returned to the capital, but others stayed put in the provinces. In the space left by my favorite restaurant, a pricey seafood eatery opened up. Throughout the city, people returned to their old habits, but there wasn't the same zest. It was as if the city had been overrun by zombies who weren't even that interested in brains anymore, so they just picked up plastic tubs of the stuff at the grocery store, dropping it in their cart without even checking the expiration date.

Bit by bit, the SDFs returned to the steps of the church down the street, encouraged by the warm weather. One of them hailed me as I went by, asking for a handout.

But this part had not changed. Cash was mostly gone for good. "*J'ai pas de monnaie,*" I told him.

"*Pas de problème,*" he replied.

I perked up.

"I have a solution," he continued in French. From his jacket pocket he pulled out a device with a few buttons and a small screen.

I stared at the thing, uncomprehending. "*Qu'est-ce que c'est?*"

He smiled. "*Je prends la carte.*"

10

Adieu

AROUND 9:00 A.M. EVERY MORNING, the crazy woman stomps down the rue Bobillot, barking and snapping at people who don't exist. Anne and I used to listen to her together at the window, and now I do it alone. The woman is tall, with ragged blond hair and dark circles under her eyes. Her cries are hard to understand—filled with words too explicit for these pages—but the tone is clearly aggrieved. I sense something eastern in the accent, maybe Slavic. There's hurt in her voice, and as her arms flail, her past springs into view. What I see is a war-torn childhood, where her mother died young, leaving her, the eldest, to raise five siblings in misery, dragging them west and north across half of Europe in search of a better life, only later to be abandoned by them all, left with nothing other than this daily march through the thirteenth arrondissement.

At least, that's the saga that comes to me as I listen to her dwindling shouts. I can take another crack at it later, for she passes several times a day, completing her rounds a little before midnight.

Turns out, the less I know about a person, the better. This is proved time and again by life in my building. In Paris, where I've had the same apartment for twenty years, I know only a handful of residents, and my ignorance about the others fuels my imagination. Who exactly *is* that man who enters the door twelve inches from mine every evening, and does he really have a wife, or is that just him holding up both sides of the conversation? What kind of doctor is it who lives on the ground floor, and why have I only seen her twice? Even Monsieur and Madame Estevès, who live in the tiny concierge apartment, are an enigma, no matter how often I speak with them.

Compare that to Minnesota, where I spend the other half of my life in a small condo building not unlike my Parisian lodgings. People there are unfailingly friendly—or, at least, chatty. By the time I finished moving in, I'd met every person in the building and could tell you how long they'd lived there, what they did in life, which way they voted, and what their dog's name was. Just like that, the mystery was gone.

In short, not knowing people somehow improves them, vesting them with special interest. It's the in-flight movie principle, according to which the best film on an airplane is by definition the one playing mutely on my neighbor's screen. There, actors gesture, they scowl, they give cutting looks, their mouths open and close, providing me with all I need to recompose the story. In one, a man and woman argue mutely in a suburban living room, and what I sense is a lifetime of heartache and the yearnings of the human soul. On another screen, three men in fatigues mouth their fears before drawing straws in a battlefield trench. In a third, a girl in a high-school hallway shrinks under a volley of put-downs, but then finds a flower in her locker. The silence is eloquent. During a transatlantic flight, I can take in several such films—sometimes visible between shoulders in the next row up—and by the time I'm done with them, they are all Oscar material. Occasionally I've decided the movie was so good that it warrants a second viewing. But when I stream it on Netflix a week later, the audio blaring, something is lost. It plods. There's none of the panache I experienced in the fuselage of the Airbus. Alas, I understand too much.

When you're at the tail end of middle age, the kids grown and your wife lost to illness, there's a lot of empty space in your head, and the population of Paris offers to fill it. The trick, I find, lies in maintaining the right distance. Stay too far away, and you miss the details that bring a person to life. Get too close, and you end up learning all about them, which renders them pretty much useless for your imagination. The gap between me and the Slavic woman in our neighborhood is ideal. She passes beneath my window on a regular basis, but we have never met.

All this came to mind one evening when I left a restaurant and entered the nearby Metro station. A young woman—twenty-something, with dark hair and a flat but pleasant face—struggled at a turnstile. She looked a bit familiar, almost like my daughter. Her problem wasn't due to her ticket, or even to the fashion police (who might well have issued a warning for the bell-bottomed jeans, which have inexplicably made a comeback). Rather, in her arms she cradled an ungainly blob of metal from which three tube-like necks arced several feet into the air, each one topped with a sphere containing a lightbulb. Her struggle reminded me of nothing more than the demi-god Hercules locked in battle with the many-headed Hydra—except that this monster was one of those standing lamps that would have looked intriguing in an Ikea showroom some years ago, only to prove itself less fit for survival outside that habitat.

Shifting right and left to angle the base through the turnstile, the young woman flicked her hair behind her ear. Her jaw was set. There was something heroic about her determination. Some people might pay to have such an object delivered, but the patches on her bell-bottomed jeans (not, I thought, purely decorative) spoke of thrift—suggesting that the luxury of delivery would outstretch this young person's finances.

Who doesn't recall those distant days when every coin counted? The scene cast me back to my own youth.

Passing through the turnstile was a no-go, so the young woman opted for the second option—the glass-paneled gate that is designed for those who find turnstiles challenging. After a mute exchange of nods and finger-pointing, the ticket agent pushed a button in his booth, and the gate clicked.

However, here, too, the bobbing skulls of the Hydra failed to pass, catching on a crossbar that threatened to lop them off. A casual observer might have applauded the decapitation of this monster—although students of classical mythology will recall how that worked out for Hercules, when two new heads sprouted from each severed neck. This evening's protagonist appeared less interested in slaying a monster than in taming it. Unfortunately, the more she pulled at the tubes, the more an unintentional beheading became likely.

This was your classic damsel-in-distress situation—which, in most circumstances, would be routinely ignored in Paris. After all, your typical local is as tough as day-old baguettes. Parisians learn from a young age that they'll never make it so far as the end of the block if they stop for everyone who needs a hand.

Luckily, the Metro plays by a different set of rules. It somehow brings out the best in folks. Some say it comes from forced proximity, as masses of travelers are funneled into the cramped spaces of stations and trains. But also, with two hundred kilometers of lines, the subway serves as a kind of connective tissue for the metropolis. As a matter of course, those of us who live, for instance, in the humble quarters of the thirteenth arrondissement have nothing but disdain for the well-heeled residents of the sixteenth, or the self-satisfied hipsters of the tenth. But the Metro bonds us. We share something—at the very least, the desire to be somewhere else—and this commonality softens us up.

Perhaps that explains the many small courtesies that occur in these spaces. One time-honored tradition concerns the baby stroller predicament. A young mother carting an infant will enter a Metro station and soon find herself at the top of a very long stairway. She hesitates. Should she attempt to descend the incline on her own? One false step, and she'll lose her balance. The stroller will slip from her grip. And then, in slow motion, you'll have a Parisian remake of the famous Odessa Steps scene in Sergei Eisenstein's *Battleship Potemkin*, with a runaway baby carriage testing its springs. But no! Before she makes her move, another passenger— usually a man—stoops before the little vehicle and picks up its front without even breaking his stride. Instantly, the mother lifts the back portion of the carriage, and together, exchanging not a syllable, the two porters carry the infant down the steps like a king on a litter, managing a four-point landing at the bottom. The man then continues on his way, expecting not a word of thanks.

Similarly, I entered a station late one evening to find a fellow in ragged clothing outstretched in the empty hallway. He looked rough, his stubble-covered cheek pressed into the asphalt. I considered tiptoeing past, but for some inexplicable reason, I stopped to ask if he was all right. He didn't budge. Then a woman came down the stairs and joined me. Together we studied him. Finally, another man showed up, and he too stopped. By turns, we nudged the fellow, once, twice, three times. We discussed what to do. The woman

pulled out her phone and dialed the French emergency number. Eventually an agent showed up and took over. The three
of us looked at one another. Had we just saved a life?

I hate to say it, but we all walk past scenes like this above
ground, where outstretched bodies seem like an unfortunate
part of the landscape—one that somebody else is supposed
to handle. In the Metro, it felt more personal. In some inde-
finable way, he was one of us.

All of which helps to explain why, at this point of the
young woman's struggles with the gate, I bounded forward
and offered a hand, tucking the spheres under the crossbar
and guiding them through.

"Ah, *merci!*" the woman cried. "*Merci!*"

Her smile, a mix of relief and gratitude, made me feel
young again. I congratulated myself on a good deed well done.

But no, the ordeal was not yet over! As we arrived on the
platform, a train was rolling in, and when the doors opened,
a new challenge arose.

Line 6 of the Paris Metro was inaugurated in 1909, at a
time when the height of the average French citizen was five
foot three. While it's true that the passenger cars have been
updated over the years, they're still not ideal for transport-
ing, say, the starting lineup of an NBA team, to which the
Hydra lamp bore an uncanny resemblance.

Worse, during a Metro stop, the average time in station runs a little over twenty seconds, and several of these
seconds had already ticked by while the young adventurer

backed through the doors, attempting to draw the bouquet of bobbing heads with her. Passengers looked up from their phones to take in the scene, but as so often happens with audiences, even when the main character is in great peril, no one offered to leap onto the stage to save her.

So, the young woman's pleading face turned back to me. Beneath her pinched brow, in the inky pools of her eyes, I saw it all. Yes, she'd picked up this ill-advised lamp for a song, probably through an online ad. It was one of many trips she'd undertaken while scraping together the necessary components for a household. Her partner was almost certainly doing the same in some other part of town—hunting for bricks-and-boards shelving, potted plants, a mattress they could throw on the floor. They were starting a life together, bound by the frayed shoestring of their budget.

I got it. I knew about hard-scrabble beginnings, from my own past, back during college, when I moved from dive to dive, upgrading from a squalid basement to a bare-naked attic. Back then, friends helped friends. Someone always had a station wagon or a pickup, and you'd take turns helping each other out—the way I once lent a hand to a girl I was falling for, where I carted boxes of books to her new place, only slightly less miserable than the last one.

Could the young woman in the Metro possibly know how important these early days would later be? They are such heady times, when you're still in the first flush of passion, stumbling into adulthood, setting up a household that isn't entirely for play. You learn how to install hooks, decorating together, discovering that electricity has a cost, and so do—who knew?—tomatoes. The first months come with a thousand small epiphanies, and they stick with you forever—at least with one of you, at least for as long as *forever* means, which is to say, as long as the past remains visible on the chalkboard of memory, mere ghostlike traces after the first wipe of the erasers of time and illness, before they are gone for good.

Alas.

Just then, the tone sounded, indicating that departure was imminent. Again I stepped forward, bundling the heads together, wrestling them down and pulling them in just as the doors closed. A few adjustments were necessary to keep the beast in check, but soon the lamp hunkered between us, its tubular necks rubbing against the ceiling of the car. As we jolted into motion, the three heads of the monster dipped and rose, as though taking a bow for their performance. The spectacle waned, and gradually the passengers returned to their own inner worlds—except for one old biddy with a finely chiseled bun who scowled at us from her seat. My partner-in-crime noticed her, too, and she turned to me, raising her eyebrows in mock alarm before giving me a wink. The death ray of the old biddy's disapproval had bonded us.

Over the clatter of the car, we chatted about how far she had to go, whether the lamp was heavier than she'd expected.

"Any second thoughts?" I asked, nodding at the giant orbs.

Her chin rose in the air and she feigned indignation. "*Je ne regrette rien.*"

It took me a moment to realize she was quoting Edith Piaf. In the famous ballad from which that line is drawn, the Little Sparrow croons about the tribulations of love, how you might turn your back on the past and make a new beginning, even late in life—one of those far-fetched ideas that I wished I could believe in.

That such a young woman would quote such an old song about old loves and old age was one thing, but what clinched it for me was that she knew I'd catch the allusion.

I liked this young person. Here she was, scraping by, composing a hodge-podge household with throwaways, and yet nothing could put a dent in her spirit. It's easy to be Hercules when you're the offspring of Jupiter, but the real heroes are the mortals.

We rolled along. One stop, two. The bobbing heads settled into a rhythm of synchronized nods. I had time to take in our surroundings.

The car was filled with your standard assortment of passengers—families, couples, a cluster of teenagers, several solo travelers. A girl with round cheeks, maybe seven years old, sat by her mother, staring at her reflection in the glass. Two young men in PSG football jerseys were rough-housing at the end of the car. Sitting erect on one of the inner seats, not far from the scowling biddy, was an older gentleman with a vacant look and a too-large suitcoat, his thin hair raked across his scalp. A homeless guy—at least I assumed he was homeless—slouched on one of the fold-down seats in the corner, his chin nestled deep in his beard, his eyes closed.

Several of the passengers were conversing, but thanks to the rumble of motion, their words were indistinguishable and thus fascinating, according to the in-flight movie principle.

Blind to class, race, and privilege, the Metro takes all comers. And like Death itself, the Metro waits for no one. It's like the sculpture of the Last Judgment on the western façade of Notre-Dame Cathedral, where, after the weighing of the souls, the damned are herded toward the cauldrons of Hell, packed as miserably as passengers during rush hour. Rich and poor, kings and laborers, each one marches grim-faced toward their fate, led by a demonic figure who wouldn't look out of place in a ticket booth.

Part Noah's Ark, part Ship of Fools, the subway conveys passengers from the cradle to the grave—and sometimes literally. It's not unheard of for babies to be born in transit, just as a few unlucky passengers will finish their greater Voyage before arriving at the end of the line. That's what makes the Metro such a feast for the imagination.

As I perused the crowd, pasts, presents, and futures appeared like thought balloons above each person's head: graduations, first jobs, moments of passion, death-bed scenes—everything was there.

I turned to take in the other side, but a glint in the glass arrested me. There stood another figure, one I had missed earlier, and that, in fact, I avoided whenever I could. It was a round-shouldered man with white hair and bags under his eyes, not as youthful as he felt, oddly unaccompanied. Before I could put a stop to it, his story, too, blossomed. The kids were there. The cats. The old house. And yes, Anne, as well, along with the summer trips, the meals, the illnesses, the weddings and funerals, the whole poorly edited movie of life. Like the Slavic woman who stalks up and down the rue Bobillot, I was encountering people who weren't there. Scenes flicked by. One by one the figures dimmed.

Behind my reflection, a ghoul floated into view, tall, stooped, and hooded—nothing missing but the scythe.

One of the Hydra heads had freed itself.

We rolled into another station, and behind me, the young woman spoke.

"*C'est ici*," she said. We had arrived.

It was time for one last battle. In a matter of seconds I'd helped her extract the tangle of necks. The orbs bobbed unbridled on the platform. I offered to help her carry the beast the last few blocks, but she declined. She had it under control. As the tone sounded, I stepped back into the car and wished her well.

The doors slid closed, and from behind the glass, the young woman with the dark hair and the flat, pleasant face raised her hand and mouthed the words *au revoir*.

I mirrored her gesture, but it was more *adieu* that came to mind—not just goodbye, but farewell, the French version, its two syllables so definitive that you never repeat them to the same person, for they announce a parting as irreversible as death itself.

As the train pulled away, I caught a final glimpse of that curious girl waddling off with the kettle-shaped base and its bobbing heads, starting her bricks-and-boards household. Hadn't I seen her before? Something echoed, as if we'd met in another time and place, when perhaps I'd also offered a hand. A tingle ran through me. It was the uncanny sensation of déjà vu.

11

Silver Screen

I'M SITTING IN ONE OF THOSE JOINTS on the rue des Écoles where they show classic movies, and the flick *du jour* is Italian with British actors, based on a short story by a French-Argentinian. It's a film about film—the kind of thing the French wet their pants for—filled with photographers, dark rooms, negatives, close-ups. A guy snapped some pictures of a girl in a park, and maybe he saw something else, too—but maybe not. To find out, he has to track her down, and when he finds her, she maybe falls in love with him—but maybe not. And maybe there was a dead body in a park—but then again, maybe not. We're getting close to the end, everything raveling and unraveling, and just as we gear up for the big reveal, the film freezes on a single frame of the guy walking in town. Suddenly the image cocks sideways, and a sash of sprocket holes runs diagonally across the screen. The image is only half-visible now, tipped to the left, and the whole picture starts to fade lighter and lighter, yellowing, going almost sepia, until a white spot appears in the middle, widening fast, the edges around it curling and melting away. The entire screen is now a wall of white. Then it stops. Cut. There's a click, and we're plunged into darkness.

Apparently, that's what passes for an ending these days.

In France they love movies like this, the ones where you have no idea what's going on. Deep down, you suspect the director didn't know either, because everything's like, *maybe this, maybe that, maybe something else.* And then, how should the story end? Who knows? In fact, here's an idea—let's make it a toss-up! Even better, why not lop the ending off altogether and let the audience do the work?

To which the American in me wants to scream a reply: *Because I paid for this! Because you went to film school and are supposed to know what you're doing. Because my days are long and hard, and when I come to the movies I want someone else to do the thinking for me. Don't make me decide if ET gets to phone home or if they're going to find Private Ryan. Put. It. On. A. Goddamned. Platter.*

Instead, we get this cop-out where, in this film about film, the actual celluloid film supposedly goes off the reel and melts in front of us, and that's the end of the story.

The house lights still haven't come up, and not a person in the audience—there are maybe twelve of us—has moved. We're sitting in the dark as an acrid smell seeps into the room. That's when we all realize the film really *did* melt. Those sprocket holes were genuine. Up in the booth, the projectionist is now bustling about, searching for scissors and tape.

Meanwhile, a conversation breaks out in the dark. People who have never met and can't see one another start talking about the movie. They like what happened—how the film about film ran headfirst into reality. How illusion met with a hot projector bulb.

And it occurs to me that maybe—just maybe—this was the best ending imaginable for a story like this.

Then again, maybe not.

Why make endings simple when you can make them complicated—that's what the French sensibility says. A few mental stretches will do no harm, and like certain yoga poses, the more contorted ones can take you to a new level. For example, you find yourself watching a film about film, and maybe even *that* film (the second one), is about another film. You've got yourself a textbook illustration of the *Petit Écolier* principle.

Let me explain. An *écolier* is a schoolboy, and if he's *petit*, he is a little one. But the littlest schoolboys in France are not sequestered in the preschool down the street. Rather, you find them at the cookie display in your local supermarket. Manufactured by the company Lu, a *Petit Écolier* is a rectangular biscuit upon which a slightly smaller slab of chocolate has been attached. It's in the chocolate part that the magic happens. If you squint, you can see there's a design embossed in the dark material—the picture of an old-timey schoolboy wearing a cape and beret. He's holding something up to his mouth, and if you zoom in on that, you can just about make out what he's eating, which is another *Petit Écolier* biscuit. This means that the treat in his hand also bears an embossed schoolboy who is, in principle, chowing down on another, identical biscuit. And so on, infinitely.

The experience of the *Petit Écolier* situation is often uncanny, making the flesh on your arms pucker. It comes up with surprising frequency in French films, but even more than that, it has to do with the entire experience of movie-going in the capital.

Why is this? For one thing, unless you have lived under a rock or were brought up by the wrong kind of cult, you have seen images of Paris a bazillion times in movies and TV shows. Often these images are real. For example, the camera shows two lovers strolling across a bridge at dusk, with a tall, metal tower—one that's shaped like a slender letter A—glinting behind them. Just such a tower truly exists in Paris, and the movie you are watching may have been shot there. On other occasions, however, no actual Paris is needed, and all you get is "Paris"—with quotation marks. In this case, the same lovers may find themselves in a café. The eatery has bistro tables with checkered tablecloths, a bar at the side, where a man in a white shirt and black vest carries a tray with wine glasses. The scene may be filmed in Peoria or Baltimore, but just like that, you've been transported to "Paris."

Watching scenes like these while you're actually visiting the city is mildly entertaining, and you feel that you yourself have become an extra in the large, ongoing movie that we live in.

But it can get creepier. For one thing, in addition to showing all the generic parts of Paris—the tower, the arc, that big museum, and all the other places that I don't even need to mention because you already know what I'm talking about—movies sometimes show parts of the city that are less well known. For instance, I was once at home watching a movie that had an edge of adventure to it. A car chase had begun, and instead of following the normal route for car chases in movies—by which I mean racing along the Seine and following the itinerary preferred by tour buses during the day—the two vehicles whizzed around the less well-known Austerlitz train station. From there, they began zooming up the Boulevard de l'Hôpital. That got my attention, for they had at that point entered the thirteenth arrondissement, typically eschewed by filmmakers for not being sufficiently photogenic. I watched wide-eyed as they reached the Place d'Italie, where the cars wheeled around that great circle, tires squealing as they passed right by the rue Bobillot, where I was currently watching. I even glanced out my window to make sure there wasn't a high-speed chase within view. But no—just a G7 taxi waiting for a client, and, on the other side of the street, a garbage truck.

Still, I experienced a shiver.

The other version of the *Petit Écolier* situation comes when you're walking in Paris, and you realize you've just entered a part of the city that you first saw on the screen. Again, it's not so surprising if it's one of the major landmarks, but sometimes people will enter the Place des Vosges, with its regal apartments lining the manicured square, or the Palais Royal, with its elegant arcades, and they will enjoy an unexpected frisson of déjà vu—all the more unexpected for having been literally seen before. The same might happen on a cobblestone street where vines creep up a wall in a particular pattern, or in a Belle Epoque brasserie. Sometimes it's a near miss, and the place you recognize never was in a movie—at least, not one that you saw. But it was close enough.

And then, when you're walking home at night, holding the hand of your beloved and gulping down the warm air of a Parisian night, you might find yourself simply dazzled, convinced that the entire city is a film set, that we are all part of the movie, great panels of light casting romantic shadows, with that thicket of people over there standing like spectators in awe of the magic being made, that man in the black turtleneck and the clipboard roaming like a producer or a gaffer or a grip, whatever they are—and look! Isn't that Jennifer Aniston?

Only to stop in your tracks and discover that it truly is Jennifer Aniston, and that you've walked into one of the umpteen film shoots going on in the city on any given day.

Paris has more movie theaters than any city in the world, and often as not, I'm sitting in one of them. But the film I'm watching is probably not French. The fact is—and I'm a little ashamed to admit it—there's a pack of French movies I can't stand. This is, after all, the country that revered Jerry Lewis, which says something disappointing about the French character. But they also have a different sense of drama. For instance, every year there are a few new movies that are always the same. You start with three couples who have known each other since high school, and now they vacation together, babysit each other's kids, etc., etc. But this summer's reunion is different. One of the six has gotten cancer, gotten divorced, gotten cancer and divorced, discovered that he/she is gay, discovered that he/she is not gay, or had an affair with one of the other people in the group. Drama, such as it is, ensues, but it doesn't ensue very far or fast. We witness a lot of hand-wringing and pensive looks. Somebody is always smoking a cigarette outside, in the dead of a sleepless night, while peering at the forest/beach/desert. I believe these movies eventually end, but my only proof of this is that when I regain consciousness, the house lights are on, and I'm the only person left.

In the US, when you get a hankering to go to the movies, the biggest question you face is, DC or Marvel? Are you in the mood for Batman or The Hulk? Wonder Woman or Captain America? Sure, they'll throw in something high-brow from time to time—a Bond or a Bourne or a Barbie—but in the international offerings you're limited to this year's bleak Irish fare or something dowdily British.

It's not as if Paris doesn't suffer from the plague of locusts that modern Hollywood produces. It does. But because there are nearly three hundred cinemas in the city, it survives the infestation. You get plenty of Spanish and German pieces, of course, along with work by the Belgians, the Italians, the Danes. But there's also recent stuff from Senegal and Morocco, Iran and Israel, China and Japan. Who needs airlines anymore when you have movie theaters?

And for those of us who feel that everyone stopped making good movies at the end of the 60's—which is my opinion three days a week—there are all the replay cinemas, like the one where the film melted in front of my eyes.

That said, it's not as if movie-going in Paris has fully resisted Americanization. The theaters have grown larger in recent times, and the seats wider. Also, people aren't as well-behaved as they used to be. It wasn't that long ago that young women ushered you to your seat in these establishments, and you offered them a small tip. People dressed up a bit, and to slump down and put your feet over the seat in front of you would have been unthinkable. These days, all bets are off. Not long ago, before she and Guy decamped to Perpignan, my friend Sabine pointed to the jacket I'd left on the empty seat next to me. "Don't do that," she said. "There are guys in the back who slide under the seats, reach up, and steal your wallet." Frankly, that one seemed a bit far-fetched. But I moved my coat.

In the past you'd be hard-pressed to buy much more than the French equivalent of Milk Duds at a movie theater. Gradually, though, the concession stands have ramped up, leading to the invasion of what Sabine scornfully describes as *les mangeurs de popcorn*, those crude individuals who plop themselves down next to you with a tub of popped and buttered kernels that they shovel into their mouth for the next twenty minutes. For Sabine, watching a movie should be akin to a religious experience, one deserving our rapt attention—uninterrupted by the sound of human cattle chewing their cud.

In France, speaking during a movie is still generally frowned upon, which is a far cry from current American habits. I recently sat through a horror movie in the States, where the audience did not seem to understand that their participation was unlikely to change the final outcome. "Watch out, buddy!" someone called as the monster crept into the frame behind the hero. "Hoo boy!" another audience member opined. "He's a goner!" And so on, until the credits rolled. It gave me a new appreciation for sitting at home with Netflix.

Silence is golden in movie theaters, and it's worth remembering that that's how it all got started. Back in 1895 the Lumière brothers screened a fifty-second sequence of a train arriving at a station—a spectacle that caused panic among the audience as the locomotive glided quietly toward them.

Not far from the rue Bobillot there's a center dedicated to movies like this, mostly ones from the 20s and 30s, where the only thing you hear (since vats of popcorn are not available on these premises) is the piano accompaniment. It's in this magical space of light and shadow that you realize how dialogue is mostly unnecessary in movies—and, in fact, in life. Little tramps, stone-faced stoics, melancholic lovers, bespectacled go-getters, one by one they march across the screen, imploring with open arms, swinging from trapeze bars, dangling from clocks, pining with their wrist pressed to their brow—all without uttering a word. The language of the body says it all—supplemented once in a while by a card announcing important transitions: "Meanwhile..."

Why, I have found myself wondering, can't real life work this way?

Which is when I realized that it can.

In my apartment, I am blessed with a large window overlooking a square that is really a triangle. Five different roadways come together here, as though my neighborhood were nothing but one large funnel, with me positioned near the spout that drains it. During my caregiving days, when the perimeter of my operations had been reduced, I'd spent hours watching the silent dramas unfolding on the other side of the glass. So, in fact, had Anne.

The plot from this vantage point is often as vague as in many French movies, but we benefit from the total absence of dialogue. No driveling about this or that. No audience members calling out warnings or offering a play-by-play. No chomping of popcorn. Just drama in its purest form, as though the neighborhood were inhabited by a very large company of mimes, and they are all on the clock. What is that little girl saying to the mother who looks so unhappy? I don't know—but I can imagine. That man who totters with two canes, one on each side—where is he going, and will he make it? I'm keen to find out. That young woman who stands with one hand on her hip while the other wags a finger at her male companion—what is she saying? What did he do to deserve it? And how will they patch things up? This, too, is a great mystery.

And for once I feel that I *am* willing to do the work. I don't need the director to serve it all up on a platter. I can figure it out and fill in the gaps. And who knows? Maybe—just maybe—I'll be able to make sense of it all.

On the other hand, maybe not.

12

French Dough

~~~~~~~

It was a Saturday morning on the rue Bobillot—time for my monthly reconciliation of debts. This process used to involve writing checks, matching them with bill stubs, stuffing them in envelopes, and rifling through my desk drawer to find another stamp or two. But during Anne's illness I had zenned my way toward maximum simplification, putting as much of my life on autopilot as possible. The only happy legacy from that long ordeal was that bill-paying had mostly become a spectator sport—one where I watched automated deposits and withdrawals volley back and forth in my accounts, rather like a slow-moving and expensive tennis match.

There were, nevertheless, a few matters to attend to manually, and one of my debts needed to be paid via a kind of transfer known as a *virement*. *Virements* are a common practice in France, and they work rather like the transporter that Scottie's team operated on *Star Trek*: money disappears from one place, only to reappear moments later in another.

When I clicked to begin the dematerialization of my funds, the portal informed me that a code would be sent to my phone to confirm the transaction.

Although these codes travel at the speed of light, I gave this one a full minute to arrive on my phone. Then two. The screen remained blank. Hoping to knock the magic numbers loose, I gave the phone a shake. The web portal offered the option to send a code again, but the second try met with the same lack of success. Something was definitely amiss. Did I have enough bars? Was I looking in the right place? I took a couple more runs at it, and finally, on the fifth try, a new message appeared on the portal.

Verrouillé. I'd been locked out.

I expect websites to wag a finger before taking drastic actions like this. A warning makes you think twice. Even my brother—way back when—used to give me a heads up about what would happen if I stepped over the masking tape separating his side of the bedroom from mine. But here they'd skipped the warning phase and gone straight to the punishment.

To make matters worse, another realization was dawning on me—namely, that the whole thing was my own damn fault. For complicated reasons, I had recently changed my phone number, and this meant the precious confirmation codes were probably going to a grandma in Alsace or a businessman in Bordeaux. What I should have done, of course, was record my new number in my account profile at the bank—the very same profile that was now inaccessible.

They say that a fool and his money are soon parted, and here was the proof of it. It had taken me less than four minutes to put my meager fortune out of reach.

The experience of being frozen out of one's bank account is a bit like hitting an air pocket on an airplane. One minute you're cruising through the stratosphere, sipping a glass of Chardonnay and spying on your neighbor's movie screen, and the next you're checking for the life vest under your seat and pounding the ceiling panel to make the oxygen mask drop down. It's that sudden realization of vulnerability—the sense that we are all, in the end, subject to the whims and caprices of fate. The smooth ride of life had hit a bump, and there's always a chance—however slight—that the jolt will trigger something larger, sending you careening from one disaster to another. I mentally patted my pockets. Did I have any cash? Were there any spare coins under the sofa cushions? In situations like this, you want a parachute.

Still, there was no call for panic. My bank is located just down the street, and on Saturdays, the branch is open till lunchtime. A solution was not far away.

The establishment where I keep my funds is known as the LCL. They used to call themselves *Le Crédit Lyonnais*, but the reference to the founding city of Lyon was no doubt deemed too provincial in our current era of globalization. This led some years ago to an exercise in rebranding—known in

French, predictably, as *le rebranding*. That term tells you all you need to know: banking in France isn't what it used to be.

Many businesses change slowly over time. At the butcher's shop, for example, we all still line up to make our selections, point to the cuts of meat we want, chat with the butcher, carry a receipt to a cashier, pay our bill, and return to the counter to collect our meat. The only change in the past fifty years is that we no longer find rabbits dangling from hooks with their fur still on.

On the other hand, banks here have changed dramatically over the past twenty years or so. Not long ago, they all had what was called a *bureau de change*—a teller's window where you could cash travelers checks or change currency, ponying up a hefty commission. And because a lot of people in France distrusted checks, and debit cards weren't yet a thing, you'd find yourself walking around with wads of banknotes every time you had a significant purchase to make. Withdrawing more than a few hundred bucks— or rather, the equivalent in francs—required several days advance notice. And all such transactions took place in a special room that was protected by bullet-proof glass, with entry through a kind of airlock security system.

But that was yesteryear. These days there's no such thing as cash in Paris—at least, not at a bank. If you visit my branch, for example, you can't withdraw a centime on the premises, and if you were to arrive with a sack full of loot ready for deposit, the staff wouldn't know where to put it. Maybe over there, by the vase of flowers? Maybe on the coffee table in the waiting area? You might be able locate an actual bank teller somewhere in Paris, but not near the rue Bobillot. There, we are now limited to *conseillers*, or advisors—a series of mostly young and always smartly dressed professionals who half-heartedly lure you toward investments you don't want and can't afford, all before they leave a month later to go to a bigger and better branch of the LCL, which is a national bank, and sees the thirteenth arrondissement as a minor league team feeding into the majors.

Long gone are the days when the advisors got to know you. In the distant past, they might even have stuck their neck out on your behalf. Many years ago, at a bank that also offered auto insurance, my *conseillère*—a bright-eyed, middle-aged woman I'd come to know rather well—had battled with underwriters to gain approval of a car insurance policy for me, which had become prickly because I didn't have a French driver's license. After long negotiations, my champion prevailed. But just as we started the paperwork, the underwriter phoned back. He had changed his mind. The policy had to be declined.

"Oh!" she cried into the phone, warning me to silence with a finger to her lips. "But it's too late! Monsieur Carpenter has already signed. He has left. He's no longer in the office." She glanced over and gave me a wink.

I don't know exactly why, but it makes you feel special when someone is willing to commit fraud for you.

Nowadays, nobody at my bank even knows who Monsieur Carpenter is. And since the recent remodeling of the branch, it feels less like a financial institution than one of your posher hair salons—the kind where sparse, uncomfortable furniture sits in a waiting room of sterile white, and a receptionist stands by a computer, ready to match you with your stylist. You're about to get a haircut, and part of it is going to be financial.

When I arrived that Saturday morning, the receptionist *du jour* wore a warm smile and primly twined cornrows. I introduced myself to the young woman, and her eyes darted instantly to her scheduling screen.

"I'm afraid I don't have an appointment," I confessed. "I'm here because I can't access my account online. It has been *verrouillé*." I explained how the codes were accumulating at my old number.

A look of faint perplexity rippled across the woman's brow, and she began clattering on her keyboard, asking for my account number, verifying my address. As she typed, she tilted her head this way and that, and when she finished, she nodded at the screen, issuing an *mmmm* sound. That's when she beckoned for a colleague, and soon a pale young *conseiller* with a shadow of beard appeared. After learning about the difficulty at hand, he graced us with a reassuring chuckle, and took over the keyboard. A few moments later, another *mmmm* was emitted.

"Your account has been locked," he informed me.

"Yes," I told him. "That's what prompted me to pay you a visit."

"I am going to send an unlock code to your phone."

I tried to tell him it wasn't going to work, but he'd already given a dramatic flourish of his French cuff and poked the Enter key. The three of us waited, exchanging looks. The man rocked on his heels. Did the situation call for small talk? We all considered the possibility. In a tacit but unanimous way we decided that small talk was not required. After a long silence, I held up the blank screen of my phone.

The *conseiller's* pert smile had gone a bit tighter now. "I see." He cleared his throat. "You will need to speak with Madame Sar, *la directrice.*"

Over the years I have worn out several directors at the LCL—the wheedling Monsieur C, the evasive Monsieur M, and the graciously ineffectual Monsieur V, for starters. Madame Sar was a new entry in the rotation.

"Happily," I said. "Where will I find her?"

"Alas! Madame Sar is not here on Saturdays," he said with a small bow, hands clasped. "You will need to return next week."

But of course.

I sometimes feel that France gets ahead of itself in the technology game. Back before World War II, they invested heavily in the concrete teeth of the Maginot Line to block a tank invasion—defenses that worked splendidly until the

Germans decided to drive around them and fly over them. Back in 1980 they created a computer network that allowed people to send messages, buy tickets online, and indulge in porn. Problem was, they didn't make it international, so it was soon edged out by a little thing called the internet. In banking, too, they are sometimes cutting edge, inventing useful gadgets like the chip card, only to get tripped up by some of the smaller and more obvious steps.

It's in this way that I soon discovered that my bank card—tied directly to the same account—was also *verrouillé*. This lesson came when I rolled my shopping cart up to the checkout in the Carrefour grocery store. A dead-eyed cashier rang up my purchases, and then the machine refused my payment. I had no cash with me, and since no one writes checks in France anymore, my options were limited. I considered making a break for it, sprinting down the street with a week's worth of groceries in my arms. But in the end, I returned each item to its original shelf under the watchful gaze of a security officer.

In the States, being cut off from my bank account would not pose a problem for several months at least. For one thing, my credit card—an invention almost unheard of in France—offers a frighteningly high limit, one designed to lure me into a never-ending cycle of debt. But I also have certain emergency resources at my disposal. I'm not talking about gold Krugerrands or hoarded toilet paper (which, if you believe the preppers, will be of roughly equal value to the Krugerrands, when push comes to shove at the latrines), but rather about the vast accumulation of pennies, nickels, dimes and quarters in the basket in my bedroom. It used to be I could bring such coins to my bank, and the teller would send them clattering in a mechanical tumbler used for sorting. You'd go in with a peanut butter jar full of small change, and leave with gas money for a month. However, now that my branch has retired the sorting contraption, coins accumulate in my home faster than *New Yorker* magazines, adding to the load on my building's joists and supporting walls. I wouldn't call it a fortune, but it's a decent plan B if you need some dough.

In Paris, though, where even your morning croissant is paid for with your debit card, coins are barely a thing anymore.

I have never been good at scrimping, but I'm also not a spendthrift, and all I have really asked of life on the financial side is to supply me with a trickle of income that will always match my needs. The past years, though, had upset that balance. In addition to snapping my life in two, Anne's disease had tested our resources. While it may have other merits, the United States of America turns out to be an expensive place to finish your existence on the planet. Setting aside the cost of the in-home help we'd needed over the years, the cozy little facility where Anne would eventually die had set me back some eight grand a month. Of course, you feel a little sheepish worrying about money while your wife's very being is slipping away—it's that uncomfortable intersection of life and livelihood. Still, when she became eligible for hospice—where she'd end up spending a surprisingly long time—I was relieved to learn that it ran only nine grand a month. That was barely a thousand dollars more than I was already paying, and for so many special services. America was great!

But no, they meant nine thousand dollars *on top of* the original eight thousand. Ah, yes, that sounded more like the America I knew. And since Anne was too young for Medicare, those costs had to come from somebody's pocket, and it looked like that somebody was me.

All this to say that now, as the dust settled, I was watching my dollars and euros more attentively than usual.

I did return to the LCL the next week, promptly at nine o'clock on Monday morning—forgetting that the branch is always closed on Mondays to make up for being open half of Saturday. On Tuesday I returned again, only to learn that Madame Sar was not "*visible*" at the moment—a term implying that a person has gone temporarily transparent, whereas in reality she is simply not available. The receptionist invited me to call her at 5:30, and when I called at 5:30, she asked me to call again the next day at 4:00, and at 4:00 the next day, the same receptionist asked me to call again half an hour later.

Finally, though, I reached the elusive Madame Sar.

"Monsieur Carpenter," she said, cutting me off half-way through my story. "This is too complicated to handle by phone. You must come in. How about…" She offered an appointment two days later.

By the time I arrived for my meeting, my account had been locked for nearly a week. I was not entirely destitute, thanks to my American credit card. However, the wire transfer I had originally needed to make was now overdue. Late charges were accruing.

The receptionist with the cornrows ushered me to a white sofa in the lounge, where I sat like a condemned man awaiting execution. I wouldn't say that I was entirely without hope, but I have met many bank directors in France over the years, and the experience did not incline me toward optimism. Thanks to the persistence of sexism in the financial sector, all the directors have been men. Thanks to the privileges of seniority, they have all been near retirement. And thanks to what used to be called the Peter Principle, which stipulates that everyone ends up promoted to the level of their own incompetence, they have all proved themselves largely ineffectual, especially when it comes to such modern practices as answering the telephone or—God forbid—responding to email. When it comes to junior executives, the kingpins of the LCL see the thirteenth arrondissement as a training ground, but for aging managers, it is more like one of those pre-slaughter holding pens where end-of-career ruminants toothlessly chew their cud before moving down the chute to the abattoir.

At the appointed hour, a beautiful young assistant with dark hair and vermillion nails collected me from the waiting area. "Monsieur Carpenter?" she said, gripping my hand and shaking it firmly. "It is a pleasure to meet you." She escorted me to an empty conference room and offered me a seat. To my surprise, she settled into the chair on the other side, where a laptop stood at the ready.

Then it hit me. This was no assistant. It was the great Oz herself! Madame Sar was no battle-ax drawn from the LCL's fossilized leadership. To the contrary, she was this attractive young person exuding competence. She was The Future.

"Monsieur Carpenter?" she said again.

I snapped to attention.

In short order I laid out my predicament, which Madame Sar grasped instantly.

"Yes," she confirmed. "In order to add your new phone number, I would need to send a confirmation code to your old number."

"Which, I think we can agree, is impossible."

"Indeed. But how else can we know if we have the real you?"

"Well," I said, "there is the fact that I'm sitting here right now. I have my passport with me, and that would seem to be a pretty good way—"

"Oh, Monsieur Carpenter," she laughed.

I didn't get the joke.

"In this case," she said, "we will need to send you a new code by post."

I was about to protest, but she'd already started typing on the laptop. The vermillion nails danced across the keys, and her confidence was catching. Against my better judgment, I began to believe. Yes, this woman was capable! Yes, a resolution to my problem was at hand!

"Voilà!" she exclaimed as a ping sounded on the computer. "The code will go out tomorrow."

Good things come, they say, to those who know how to wait, so I waited intensely.

In my building we have no mailboxes, which means that Madame Estevès, the concierge, handles all the mail for some fifty households. It gets delivered to her in a bundle, and she then makes the rounds, one floor after the other, sliding envelopes under the door. If a package has arrived, or there's something to sign for, she leaves a special notice inviting us to collect it at her tiny apartment, where she is almost never to be found because she's so busy with the lengthy mail distribution, along with her cleaning chores. Over the next few days, around ten a.m., the floor would creak outside my door as Madame Estevès did her mail round. Then it would creak again as she moved on without sliding anything under my door.

During this long interlude, I survived by withdrawing money from the ATM on my US account. This was not exactly a hardship, but in the post-currency world that Paris had become, gigantic fifty-euro notes—the denomination favored by the machines—were hard to pass off, especially when you mostly wanted a one-euro baguette for dinner or three euros for a chunk of cheese. The secret about Paris is that it's not that expensive to live in—at least, not once you get away from the hotels and restaurants and museums and monuments that plug up the tourist area. In my neighborhood, I spend less on groceries than I would in the States, and I can buy them in smaller quantities. Rather than acquiring whole gunny sacks of fruits and vegetables, I pop over to the little shop across the street and choose a couple of carrots and a radish—whatever is needed for the job at hand. This was another place where fifty-euro bills were unwelcome.

Lots of people are nostalgic for the old currency. Banknotes in francs used to be adorned with portraits of famous French people—writers, artists, philosophers, you name it. The euro bills have no faces on them at all. Instead, they show architectural motifs—doors and windows on one side, and old-fashioned bridges on the other. Everywhere in the eurozone the bills are the same, and the artwork is deliberately vague. Your average French person assumes they're looking at a picture of the pont du Gard bridge in Provence, whereas an Italian assumes the same picture shows an aqueduct closer to Rome. In this small but subtle way, the bureaucrats of the European Union work to fool us into thinking that we are all the same.

It's when you don't have something that you notice it the most. The secret code that I required persisted in not arriving, and this was a great puzzle. My building lies just a few hundred yards from the LCL, and you might be excused for thinking that the mail would come rather swiftly. That said, any letter would no doubt be routed first to some sorting facility in central France before boomeranging its way back up here. And, in fact, the code was almost certainly not issued by the branch office in the lowly thirteenth arrondissement. No, it would have been generated in a computer center in Frankfurt or London, then to be sent to the sorting facility, afterwards to arrive at the local post office, where the mailwoman would add it to the stack in her cart, only to hand it off later that day as part of the bundle she gave to Madame Estevès, who would then leave a note under my door inviting me to come down and sign for it.

Five days later, I returned to pay a visit to Madame Sar. She expressed surprise that I hadn't received the code, and while I watched, her fingernails—now a dark sea-green that complemented the hue of her skin—flew again over the keyboard.

"But it is right here," she said, gesturing at the screen.

She turned the computer to share the view, and there it was: an utterly unambiguous request that a new code be sent to my address—in Minnesota.

It hadn't seemed necessary to me, back when I was sitting across the table from her, to point out that I was not currently in the United States.

"But that is the official address of your account," she protested.

"Would it not be possible for me to receive it at my apartment at the rue Bobillot?"

"You mean, to *change* your address?"

"That's right."

"Of course. But to do so, we will need to send a code—"

I raised a hand to stop her. I knew where she was headed, and I didn't want to hear it.

While I waited for the code to arrive in the US—where I had a friend ready to intercept it—I pondered life. There's a great paring down that occurs when you lose a spouse. Accounts get revised. Your tax status changes. Somehow even the spammers get wind of it, for Anne's email account had gone all but dormant, and even the flow of junk mail had slowed. It occurred to me that a much larger task lay before me, too: I would need to have her name removed from the title of the apartment—a task of dizzying complexity that would make me nostalgic for the days when my greatest concern was a missing code.

And then, what about when my own time came? Was I going to leave the whole, messy business to Paul and Muriel? People have been dying, on again off again, ever since the first homo sapiens dropped down from a tree and broke his neck. It seems like an oversight that we haven't figured out how to simplify the exit.

The code never did show up in the US. Probably it had been sent by hot air balloon. All in all, more than three weeks elapsed before I made the trek back down to the LCL.

Apparently another great rotation had occurred in the agency. The receptionist with the cornrows was gone, replaced by a pale boy with an Adam's apple the size of a golf ball. He looked like a kid who has just been pulled away from his Play Station for the first time in a decade. When I asked to see Madame Sar, he apologized, explaining that she was not *visible*.

"Is there anything I can do to help?" he squeaked, the golf ball bobbing up and down.

"No," I sighed. "It's a problem with my phone number, you see…"

And step by step, I took him through it—the highs and lows, the twists and turns, backwards and forwards, regaling him with the details of my epic struggle. The whole time, he poked away at his computer.

"I see," he said.

"And that's just the beginning." On I went.

"*Mmmm*," he murmured, imitating his predecessors while he peered at the screen. "Maybe we could—"

PARIS LOST AND FOUND

"They've tried everything."

"Still, I think it's possible—"

"Hang on." I raised my hand to halt him. My phone had just dinged, and I dug it out of my pocket. A text message had rolled in. It showed a number with six digits. What the hell was this?

"There you go," the young man said. "I just sent you a code."

13

Scaredy-Cat

SPEAKING OF DEATH, THE FUNERAL HOME down on the rue de Tolbiac went out of business.

It wasn't one of the full-service establishments like we have in the States—those long one-story buildings with a back entrance for hearses and an assembly room up front, both of which communicate with the sales space kept curtained to the side. No, this was just a *pompes funèbres* boutique, tucked between the Century 21 and a computer repair store. Such enterprises in the US tend to have sober-sounding names like McReavy & Horn, or Gates of Heaven. This one was part of a chain called EurObsèques, a telescoping of the words for *Europe* and *funerals*, kind of along the lines of AmericInn or Interpol. At EurObsèques you could choose urns and ponder arrangements, but the lion's share of the work would be done off the premises.

It's been a tough economic climate for everyone, but still, if there was such a thing as a bullet-proof business plan, it seemed like EurObsèques had it: prime placement in the middle of a decent neighborhood, and a steady customer base. Was it possible they'd had too much competition? There are four other *pompes funèbres* within walking distance, but these had never struck me as cut-throat enterprises, the kind that ran specials or waged price wars.

Alas, nothing is forever. Not even the job of selling eternity.

Let me start by saying that death sucks. Or even, to apply an intensifier that was popular in my youth, it sucks *eggs*. I've heard all the counter-arguments from the philosophers and fanatics. It's nothing, it's a better life, it's a higher plane. Yada yada yada. I don't dispute any of these claims, since there aren't a ton of reviews on the topic. It's not like you can google "death" and see that everyone who tries it gives it three-and-a-half stars. What I'm attempting to express is that it sucks eggs *for those of us who are still here*.

You don't get to my age without leaving a trail of carnage behind you. People peel off, one by one, and while I'm generally glad not to be dead myself (although, see above—how would I know?), it's not great being left behind, either. It doesn't help when your friends have moved away. And if your kids have careers and partners, you find yourself thinking that you don't want to be a burden to anybody else, so you just settle in and become a burden upon yourself.

The closure of the EurObsèques boutique reminded me that I was late for my pilgrimage—a semi-regular trip to one of the local cemeteries. A poet I like is buried there, and for the past three decades I've been making house calls from time to time to drop off a few flowers.

There's a florist's shop on the ground floor of my building, and it's run by a wisp of a woman who is second-generation Vietnamese. Her tiny crevice of a store teems with bouquets and house plants, everything from your hardy succulents to those fussy orchids. I popped in and grabbed a few yellow roses.

"She'll be very happy with those," the woman said.

"They're for a *him*, actually," I told her

The comment triggered a suppressed double-take, and I saw what was running through her head. She'd seen me come and go in this building for over a decade, and it must have just occurred to her how long it had been since she last saw Anne. Years! And now, here I was, buying a bouquet for a man.

Who can claim to understand the secrets of the human heart?

I considered correcting her, but that was liable to make things worse. And besides, she was just about to strip off the thorns from the stems. The poet whose tomb I was going to visit was not likely to prick his fingers on anything—and besides, he was a fan of all that stung and cut.

"Oh," I told her, "you can leave those on."

Her lips pulled back, as if she'd just eaten a bug. Who knows what scene of thorn-filled S&M flashed through her mind?

The cemetery is a fair distance away, over in the fourteenth arrondissement. There aren't many of them in the capital, so it's always a hike to get to one. In general, France prefers to centralize things—which is why Paris is plopped in the middle of the country, a colossal beating heart, with all the rail lines and highways converging on it like arteries. That's also true for how the country has dealt with its dead citizens, at least until recently. Here in the city there used to be one mammoth funeral home, the size of an Ikea, up in the nineteenth arrondissement. A hundred and fifty processions would depart from there daily, and they had a fleet of 80 hearses. These days the mortuary work has been spread out a bit, so that every time you turn around there's another funeral home in front of you—places like EurObsèques. In addition to their bricks and mortar storefronts, these chains also run their own websites, and you can even shop online, adding things like "*incinération*" to your cart (currently 1640 euros), before plugging in your discount code and choosing your payment method.

On the cemetery front, though, it's hard to fully decentralize things, partly because it's tricky divvying up a client base after those clients have been planted. You'll find twenty different choices in Paris, but most of them are mom-and-pop operations. The real volume is handled by a few big boys. Père-Lachaise is the one that gets all the press, but my destination was the *Cimetière Montparnasse*, the most densely populated area of the left bank, and the only one where your neighbors don't make any noise at all. Why? Because they are *dead*.

Dead. Death. Die. In English, we don't like to use these words. In the US, people don't die, they "pass away," as if they've gone on a long vacation and—who knows?—might come back. You can take the dramatic route and say that they *perished*, or use the lawyerly *deceased*, or the ministerial *departed*. Or you can let it fly, saying that they *croaked*, they *met their maker*, *kicked the bucket*, *gave up the ghost*, *cashed in their chips*, or *bought the farm*. French has its own collection of colorful expressions. Here, in addition to surrendering your soul, you can *snap it, swallow your birth certificate, eat dandelion roots, carry your rifle on the left*, or *break your pipe*.

It was the last of these expressions—*se casser la pipe*—that came up in a story Cyril had told me at a time when the building committee had reached a low point, which is to say a period when there were pitifully few emergencies, leaving time for small talk. His anecdote had to do with his father, who had studied philosophy in Paris, writing his dissertation under a director he revered so much that he began to imitate him, even taking up pipe smoking. The director was named Hippolyte, and he was such a buddy to Cyril's dad that he offered his student a beautiful pipe, just like his own, as a graduation gift.

Many years later, then living hundreds of miles from Paris, Cyril's father had established his own career as a professor. One day, during a contemplative smoke with the treasured gift, he fumbled it, and the pipe hit the floor, breaking in two.

That very same day, he received an email from a friend in Paris who had sad news to impart. "*Hippolyte s'est cassé la pipe,*" the friend wrote. He was dead.

The story made my flesh tingle.

When I was a kid, tales like that worked like today's energy drinks—there was no chance at all I'd sleep for the next twenty-four hours. For that reason, my older brother relished telling me ghost stories. For a while we shared a room with bunkbeds, where I was relegated to the exposed upper deck—the one that stood at a convenient height for any murderers or vampires who happened to be passing by. After lights out, I would clench my eyes shut, hoping to launch myself into sleep. But usually Jeff started talking before I managed to drop off, and soon we'd be in the midst of classic tales. *Thump, Thump, Drag,* was one of his favorites, and he crafted innumerable variations, especially on nights when we had a babysitter. Another one was called *The Hook.* At that age, Jeff was not what you would call an avid reader, but searching for inspiration, he began working his way through the short stories of Edgar Allan Poe. Soon my nights were filled with pits and pendulums and belfries.

Whenever I cried out for Mom, he whispered one word: *scaredy-cat.*

She would barge into the room, as fearsome as any ghoul. There'd be a storm of accusations and denials, and finally she would sentence us both to silence.

"If I hear another word…" she'd say, wagging her finger in a manner that made finishing the sentence unnecessary.

The door would close, sealing us once again in our bedroom crypt. After a minute or two in the dark, I could sense it. I knew it was coming. And then, sure enough, barely audible from the bunk below there came a wordless two-beat pulse. *Uh-uh.* A couple seconds later, it sounded again. *Uh-uh.* And it continued, like a clock ticking, *Uh-uh. Uh-uh.* I could hear the croaking pulse more distinctly now. *Uh-uh! Uh-uh! Uh-uh!* The sound was growing—hark! louder, louder, *louder.* And then I was sure: It was the beating of his hideous heart!

Jeff would dissolve into laughter.

Little did I know that our bedroom configuration back then was eerily similar to how Parisian cemeteries work. Plots are priced by the surface area here, just like other real estate, and if you calculate by the square meter, it costs more to be dead in Paris than alive, depending on the neighborhood. Because space is at a premium, higher density accommodations are attractive from a price perspective. In the metropolis this is accomplished by building upwards. Eight or ten stories isn't unusual. In cemeteries, too, verticality has its advantages, although when you're dealing with a grave, people tend to go the other direction, digging down. In this way, it's not uncommon to have bunkbeds in the vault, or even bunkbeds on top of bunkbeds, some of them going down several layers.

It's a family affair—along with grandmas and grandpas, and maybe even *their* grandmas and grandpas.

Looking back, I feel sorry for Jeff that he hadn't known about this style of tomb back when he was composing stories in our room at night. Yes, I'd have been the one to suffer, but it would have made him so terribly happy.

Back in ancient Greece they had this idea that lifespan was determined by the Fates. One of these creatures would measure out the thread of your life, and the other would snip it with her shears, and that's how much you got. Twelve inches for some, fifteen for another. And, of course, you didn't know until you got there.

But sometimes it's doled out in different ways.

A few years ago, a friend of mine retired from his teaching job at the age of fifty-eight. I was surprised that he would bail so early.

"Well," he said, "you know the story about my dad."

I did. His father—also a teacher—had retired from his position at 63. And four months later, he died of a massive heart attack.

"I'd like to enjoy a bit more retirement," Ian told me.

It seemed alarmist to me, but who was I to say? They threw a little party, and he started working on his golf game while drawing his pension.

Four months later he dropped dead from a massive heart attack.

No, the Fates don't always measure the thread from birth. Ian was simply destined to die four months after retirement.

Let that be a lesson.

Which brings to mind one of the world's most famous scaredy-cats.

In 1904, the sculptor Auguste Rodin made his first casting of *The Thinker*. Everyone knows this statue of a naked man hunched over in thought. He looks like he's been given a tricky math problem to work out, or is maybe trying to remember if he turned off the stove before leaving home. In fact, though, he was designed to sit at the top of a whopping big sculpture called The Gates of Hell, showing scenes of the afterlife. There he looks down at swirling vignettes of torture and grief, with some pretty miserable souls clawing their way out of graves and scrambling over their own children to get out. A few have made their way to the top, about to escape, only to lose their grip and fall back into the stew below.

And the whole time, you know that the hunched thinker at the top, perched like a kid on a bunkbed, listening to stories he doesn't want to hear, is thinking one thing, and that's *Holy crap*.

You can't really blame him for being worried, because the hereafter looks like even more of a mess than the here-and-now.

Sculptures are still a thing in France, at least in the cemetery department. Even at the branch offices of EurObsèques they offer some simple marble options. If you don't mind buying off the rack, an angel or cherub won't set you back too much. If money is no object, you can go full-on Gates of Hell. Most people choose something in between.

At cemeteries in the States, upright tombstones are standard fare, sometimes decorated with an ivy engraving. In France, unless they go for one of those shack-like crypts, they tend to start by slapping down a slab of marble, using that as a pedestal for everything else. At the Montparnasse cemetery, where I finally arrived with my wilting roses, you find plenty of tombs laden with artwork. Sometimes it's just a likeness of whoever broke their pipe, often in the form of a bust or a small medallion. But there's no shortage of full-sized angels of mercy, couples locked in an embrace, princely lions, grieving widows—not to mention a bunch of one-offs, like an alligator, a centaur, and a six-foot-tall multi-colored cat.

The tomb I was headed for belongs to Charles Baudelaire, an unhappy poet of the nineteenth-century who got his start translating the very same Edgar Allan Poe stories that my brother used for terrorizing me.

I entered the grounds early in the morning, which is unquestionably the best time to be in a cemetery. For one thing, that's when it's mostly empty—not counting, of course, all the permanent residents. You might find an old woman filling up a watering can before she visits her husband's grave, and that's often the hour for service vans to deliver wreaths. If you're really lucky, you'll catch the *chink, chink, chink* of an engraver chiseling in the date and name of some recent arrival.

On the east side of the Montparnasse cemetery there's a hefty sculpture of Baudelaire, and that's where a lot of people look for him. It's a tall, cream-colored block featuring a brooding figure who resembles one of the pensive demons on Notre-Dame Cathedral. But that's not actually where the poet is buried. The grave is on the other side of the cemetery, and you need to make your way along narrow paths to get there. On your way you'll probably bump into a haughty granite tomb that also has Baudelaire's name on it. This one isn't his, either. It stands to honor the former (and expired) presidents of the Baudelaire fan club, who, if they formed a fan club and then erected a glorious monument to themselves, rather sadly missed the point.

That's because Baudelaire didn't go in much for the grand and haughty. He was responsible for shattering French poetry in the middle of the nineteenth century, and then making something new out of it. Pushing away the verses of his time, which had become rather moody and lugubrious, he jammed together surprise, hate, terror, love, history, humor, and all that is ugly or beautiful, creating a distillation of Paris:

> *Teeming city, city full of dreams,*
> *Where phantoms jostle in the light of day!*
> *Everywhere, mysteries seep like sap*
> *Through the narrow canals of the*
>   *mighty colossus.*

Still, as the saying goes, no good deed goes unpunished, and in exchange for his transformation of French literature, life rewarded Baudelaire with money troubles, drug addiction, poor health, an oppressive step-father, a ban on his most famous book, fines he couldn't pay, syphilis, a scathing hatred of the common and banal, all leading up to the stroke that reduced the most articulate man in France to a single phrase—translated roughly as "Fucking hell!"—before finally rubbing him out completely at the age of 46.

And in case the message *still* wasn't clear, the Fates—the ones who measured and snipped the thread of his days—made sure he ended up in this particular cemetery, in a tomb that he would have to share for all eternity with the stepfather he loathed.

Talk about being grounded by your dad.

It's a small grave, tucked behind a couple others. The mini-obelisk has seen better days, and it tips a bit to the left. There are no sculptures or likenesses, and for me, that's handy, because this is the tomb where I keep all my dead, at least mentally. It's the bunkbed scenario, all over again, and the layers go way down. Yes, Baudelaire is there, but he scoots over and makes room for the others—my grandparents, my uncles and aunt, my dad, my brother, my sister, along with the parade of others, Tom and Barbara and Ian and Rich and Carol and Ross and Charles, and so many more.

And Anne? Yes, she's there, too. What else can you do but lay them all to rest, stop by from time to time, and tip your hat? And then, as best you can, move on.

I stood, hunched and thinking, pondering it all. It's not great being on this side of life when everyone else is gone. But what's the rush? Soon enough we'll each break our pipe, and someone will order our *incinération* on the EurObsèques website, settling up with PayPal.

The present isn't always great, but the long-term future is far from rosy. Overall, my conclusion hasn't changed. Sucks. Eggs.

And then, from somewhere, ever so softly, I hear it.

Uh-uh.

A bit louder.

Uh-uh. Uh-uh.

And also faster.

Uh-uh. Uh-uh. Uh-uh.

No, it's not Jeff down in the bunkbed, taking the opportunity for one last gotcha. If only it were. No, the tell-tale sound is too close and loud. I glance to my left and right, but there's no one else. Which is when I realize it's my own heart pounding, and now beginning to race.

Why? Because I'm such a goddamned scaredy-cat.

14

A Thing I Saw: Signs

THROUGH THE MUDDLE OF PARKGOERS, near the edge of the pond, a flash of black, a wing. A dark swan had waddled out of the water and now stood like a bully in the middle of the path. Famously elegant when gliding across a glassy surface, these creatures—called *cygnes* in French—hulk when on dry land. The one in question had the heft of a bulldog on duck legs, and it craned its orange bill toward passersby, who gave the animal a wide berth, knowing perhaps the penchant of these birds for violence. Like ballerinas, under their tutu of feathers swans are all muscle, strong enough to break bones. Recently a murderous one had pecked twenty of its fellows to death in a Welsh moat.

Then, from nowhere, a small girl appeared, maybe three years old, somehow unattended. Her waddle resembled that of the bird, which watched her as she approached. Soon they were eye to eye. The girl's mouth hung open with wonder.

She began to raise her hand, as though to pet the long neck, which drew back, forcing her to lean in even closer.

I'm no David Attenborough, but like others who document the goings on of our little globe, I typically adhere to the principle of non-intervention. Yes, it's hard to watch a cheetah take down that adolescent zebra, but it's the way of the world. Now, though, I had no stomach for a goring, and none of the other zebras were paying any attention at all.

As I stepped forward, a gloved hand caught my elbow. It was an old woman in a wool coat. Like me, she was watching the spectacle, and as I began to explain the danger, she cut me off.

"Not this one," she breathed. "She's gentle."

Turns out the swan's partner had sung his song over a year ago, and for months now this one, the surviving member of the couple, circled the little pond alone at her stately pace, dressed in widow black.

The girl leaned farther. For a moment it seemed she might tumble into the bird, but then she caught her balance, and her small fingertips stroked the feathers at the base of the neck. The animal raised its bill and closed its eyes.

Swan. It's one of the rare words that looks like what it is, the neck of the S curving up and over, leading to the beaked serif overlooking its own body with the double wings. In French, *cygne* is pronounced like another word, so that this bird is also always a *signe*, a sign.

15

Shot in the Dark

I WAS SITTING IN THE LIVING ROOM when a man's voice echoed from the street below. For some reason, it stood out from the ordinary din of the rue Bobillot—that medley of revving engines, squealing brakes, and tooting bus horns. It's not as though a voice is unexpected in these parts. After all, there are plenty of pedestrians going by, and you also get the squawking of rogue parakeets in the Linden trees, punctuated by the bangs and booms of the daily garbage pickup. Come to think of it, there's quite a bit of noise. When you least expect it, a guy with a battered trumpet struts by belting out rounds of *When the Saints Go Marching In*, and when you least want it, the furry Corsican in the insurance agency sits outside, practicing his guitar. The cherry on top of this sundae of clamor comes with the glass recycling truck. Whenever it dumps a ton of bottles into its bin, the crash crescendos like a building collapse.

That said, once you're used to all the ruckus, it's only the oddball stuff that sticks out. The tinkling of a small bell might catch your attention, and a moment of utter silence would be absolutely alarming.

Some such novelty inflected the voice below my window, rendering it unusual. The man sounded gruff—in fact, angry. I don't know what tremor of the vocal cords indicates that violence is imminent, but that's what I detected.

We were in the month of May, on one of the zillion or so holidays that fall during the spring, which meant the only store open for business today on our ground floor was the bakery. Were people coming to blows over the last croissant? Or had some other injustice regarding baked goods been committed?

I opened my window and leaned over the balustrade, the way you sometimes crane for a view from a box at the theater.

Some forty feet below, three men stood next to broad panels blocking the road. Two of them—one skinny, the other pudgy—wore the orange vests and badges that brand a person as a city worker. But it was the third one who occupied center stage. He was bigger than the other two, and he trembled with energy, his black pullover sliding over a muscular frame. This fellow was unshaven—not in the slovenly way I sometimes am, but in the trim and fit way that has become fashionable among the trim and fit. He barked at the men in the vests, poking his finger at them, gesturing first at the barrier, then thumbing back at a Mercedes convertible that idled a few feet away.

All at once, I got it.

It will be useful to know that in recent years the mayor of Paris has attempted to improve life in the capital by closing certain roads to cars. However, in some areas, like mine, the closures are sporadic. The logic our city leader has applied for these closures has no doubt been optimized by a bevy of mathematicians, but for the layperson it has proven challenging to understand. The system is mysterious. In my neighborhood, for example, several streets are closed to automotive traffic on some—but not all—Sundays and holidays, and many of us have failed to deduce the pattern of closures. Is it only the first, second, and fourth Sundays of each month? Or is it just on Sundays where the date is also a prime number? We simply don't know, and this makes it hard to guess where—or even if—to park your car.

The closures themselves are unambiguous. They are signaled by large yellow panels that spring up overnight like mushrooms—if mushrooms could be large enough to block traffic.

The mayor's plan has unquestionably succeeded at keeping cars from entering the neighborhoods in question. However, the taskforce of mathematicians overlooked that they were, by the same stroke, imprisoning motorists who were already parked in these areas. This kind of problem was long ago identified by the musical group known as the *Eagles*, who sang of a very welcoming hotel you can never leave. Our mayor, however, outdid the *Eagles* by proposing a solution to the problem. After closing the streets with giant panels, agents in orange vests would remain next to them, converting them from barriers into checkpoints. When some inmate from inside the zone needed to leave, the agents could swivel the panels to allow their escape. Because the shifts for this work are long, and the number of people needing to get out is small, folding chairs are provided for the agents to sit on while they scroll through their phones all day.

This is the kind of thing my property taxes cover in the City of Light.

On the morning I'm describing, no one was trying to break out of the pedestrian zone. Instead, the burly driver in the black pullover was attempting to go against the grain, and *enter* it. The vested sentinels were refusing to allow him to do so. The conversation was a bit hard to follow at first (at the theater, too, you sometimes wish they'd speak up for those of us in the cheap seats), but luckily the volume rose as the exchange grew more heated. As far as I could make out, the burly fellow lived in the neighborhood—or else had something to pick up in one of the streets.

The skinny agent patted him on the shoulder as though to calm him, but the man wrenched himself away. "Don't you touch me!" he bellowed in French. "Don't you touch me!" And then, surprisingly, he leaned back in, fists clenched. He turned the phrase around. "You wanna touch me?" He turned again, going nose to nose with the pot-bellied one. "Go ahead—just touch me! Just touch me!" It smacked of that scene from *Taxi Driver* where a young Robert De Niro dares his mirror to admit that it's looking at him.

This kind of taunting has a way of backfiring. Nothing makes you want to do something more than being told not to do it. It's like warning kids not to lick a metal pole during the winter because their tongue will stick there. When I was little, none of us had ever dreamt of doing such a thing, but after we received the warning, nothing was more tempting.

Predictably then, the pudgy agent *did* touch the guy, and this triggered bedlam. I have always taken "hopping mad" to be a figure of speech, but here it was playing itself out before me. The burly guy rocked on one foot, then the other, his arms curved like parentheses above his head. Out of nowhere, two other agents emerged, including a boss-like one whose bald spot shone up toward me. The more they tried to calm the man down, the more enraged he became.

I'm not sure why, but the scene below felt un-French. I don't mean to suggest that Parisians don't argue. They do. In fact, they're famous for it. When I have students doing homestays in the capital, it's not uncommon for them to take me aside after the first day or two and say they need to be moved because their host parents are getting a divorce. They know this because of the violent arguments taking place over the dinner table. A little research invariably reveals that the marriage has never been stronger. That was no squabble. It was what the French call *une discussion*. They're just more energetic about discussions than Midwesterners.

That said, the scene unfolding on the rue Bobillot had escalated beyond the impassioned debate for which the French are famous. We had roared past the level of mere hot tempers and were approaching the brink of actual rage.

Then it happened. The unshaven maniac bounded back to his car. Because it was a convertible, I could see him lunge across the front seat, his body writhing as though he was wrestling a boa constrictor. He groped about, searching. There seemed to be a bag on the floor of the passenger seat. Then he went for the glove box.

All at once I thought: *Hoo boy.*

One of the agents had lit up a cigarette. The others were chatting. How did they not see what was coming? I tried to shout out a warning, but all I could make was a croaking sound. Where was our trumpet player when we needed him? Even the Corsican guitar music might have helped.

There's a well-known principle in storytelling called *Chekhov's gun.* Attributed to the Russian writer Anton Chekhov, it asserts that once a firearm has been introduced at the beginning of a tale, it had darn well better be used by the end of it.

While I have always admired this as an esthetic rule, I have regretted its broad application on the stage of real life, especially in my homeland. In the US there are lots of disputes that go off the rails. You could be in a kerfuffle about who's sleeping with whose spouse, or whether a certain borrowed shovel was ever returned, and tempers start to flare. A vague sense of foreboding seeps in. Things veer out of control. An argument of this sort is like a string of firecrackers. There's always a chance it will sputter out, but more than likely, as each quip explodes, it sets of the next one, and the next, so on and so on, until it reaches a fevered pitch, a climax, and then—who saw it coming?—some idiot pulls out a gun.

That's when your heart sinks, because you know full well that one of you is going to end up dead, and seeing how you're the unarmed one, it's probably going to be you. Drama itself demands it. You start wishing you had a gun of your own.

And then, because you're in America, you remember that you *do* have one. Woohoo!

The dynamics tend to be a little different in France, where guns aren't as much of a thing. I don't mean they don't have firearms here. It's not as if every dispute is settled by rock-paper-scissors. To begin with, there are a million hunters in the country, and they're not restricted to using the Vulcan Shoulder Pinch to subdue their prey. A friend of mine, Philippe, is armed for this sort of thing. He loves to don camouflage outfits and stalk through the woods before blowing away wild pigs. But outside of the sporting community, guns aren't so common. In all my years in Paris, I've only known one person to have been mugged at gunpoint— and to be perfectly honest, he was kind of asking for it.

Anyone who has visited Paris in recent years know how much the police like to strut about with compact assault rifles, but firearms of the illegal variety are hard to come by. Some years ago a gritty movie came out where the entire story revolved around a revolver—one that had fallen into the wrong hands. That pretty much tells you what you need to know. Basically, in France, one measly gun goes missing, and they call it a drama, whereas in the States we call it Tuesday, or Wednesday, or any other day of the week.

It was actually a Friday, about a year ago, when I had my last gun encounter in the States. I was taking my Subaru in for an oil change, and as I zipped along the interstate, my phone rang. It was the service rep at the dealership, asking if we could reschedule.

"But I'm almost there," I whined. "I'm like,"—and here I exaggerated a bit—"two minutes away."

"Oh," he said. "I see." There was a pause. "Problem is, we have a bit of a situation on our hands." He was sorry to inconvenience me.

"What kind of situation?"

"At the moment, the dealership is surrounded by cops."

"By what?" I said.

"Well, police cars."

I waited for an explanation. After all, it seemed unlikely they were all there to get their tires rotated. In the end, I had to ask.

"Oh," he replied, "there's some guy with a rifle on the roof of the Goodwill next door."

I waggled my head so hard that my cheeks flapped. "Did you say *rifle*? Has anyone been shot?"

"Oh, no. Nothing like that."

"Are you sure?"

"So, how about Monday morning? Or better, Tuesday? Would Tuesday work for you?"

I gave it a thought. If they ended up with a mass shooting, they might need an extra day to mop up the blood.

"Great," he replied. "Tuesday it is. We'll see you then."

And he wrapped up by wishing me a nice day.

Down below, in the street, the man had stopped writhing. His hand had landed on something in the glovebox. Whatever he was looking for, he'd found it, and he started pulling himself upright.

Meanwhile, the guys in vests loitered by the barrier. A couple of them were still scrolling through their phones. Two of them chatted—one muttering something with a wry smile as his partner chuckled. The boss had just lit another cigarette and took a long drag, evidently bored out of his bald skull. None of them paid any attention to the lunatic scrambling from his car.

I'm not exactly one of those people who grew up with guns. I didn't spend my childhood in a duck blind or earning myself a deerstalker hat. But my brother Jeff and I did learn how to blast away clay pigeons with a shotgun. That was my dad's idea of fun. He'd grown up in a farm community, and on Friday nights they liked to go out to the town dump and pick off rats. For some reason, he thought it important that we learn to shoot, but my only real hunting experience ended with a dead squirrel that no one was even going to eat. I hung up my vest after that.

My experience with handguns came decades later, after Dad passed away. Going through his house, I found a loaded revolver under his bed, another in a kitchen drawer, and a rifle in the front-hall closet—positioned for easy grabbing in case the house was assailed by terrorists or Jehovah's witnesses. There were thirty-one firearms in all, ranging from a Belgian dart pistol to a semi-automatic rifle, along with crates of ammunition. I wondered briefly if Dad had secretly been a survivalist, but if so, he wasn't a very good one. The freezer, for example, was stuffed with half-eaten orders from White Castle, whereas the preppers prefer their meat canned or cured.

In the States there are more firearms than people, so in this respect—as in so many others—I fall below the national average. That said, I'm not *that* far below. Four or five years ago, after the nation was rocked by one of the larger mass shootings of the month, I bought myself a handgun to try to understand why these things were so infatuating for one half of my compatriots and so infuriating for the other. I wasn't sure what effect gun ownership would have. Would I feel safe with a deadly weapon within reach? Or would the sheer deadliness just make my own fears worse?

My earlier contact with Dad's arsenal hadn't prepared me for the experience of acquiring a gun for myself. That process provided the strange mix of excitement and apprehension you feel when a roller coaster approaches its peak, and you wonder if it's too late to get off. It began with the application for a permit, which I filled out at my local police station in the company of several officers who, not having been dispatched that day to a Subaru dealership or any other crime scene, had nothing better to do than watch civilians like me who wished to arm themselves. My fingers trembled so much that the form was nearly illegible, but luckily no one was that interested in deciphering the document. Rubber-stamp all the way. *Voilà!* I was now authorized to exercise my God-given right to put myself and others in danger.

I did my shopping at a bunker-like enterprise that advertised itself as the biggest gun shop in the Midwest. A sturdy woman named Sandy showed me an endless series of Glocks and Rugers. Some were too heavy, some too light. There was a cute little Beretta that felt like a fashion statement. Then she slid a snub-nosed Smith & Wesson in front of me, and my heart pounded. It was a six-shooter that wouldn't have been out of place in a Western. Beautifully machined, just the right heft. The cross-hatching of the grip matched the lines on my palm.

After the purchase, Sandy offered me a brochure for some of the events the shop regularly hosts. Beyond your run-of-the mill contests and trainings, there were occasional shoot-'em-up days that worked a bit like the obstacle courses we did in junior high, except that these took place in the countryside, on a parcel of land studded with old mobile homes and junker vehicles. At one station, you'd be seated on a school bus filled with kid-sized mannikins, and when you're least expecting it, the cardboard cutout of a hostage-taker would bob in from the door. Your job would be to blast that sucker to Kingdom Come. In another, you'd be lying in a bed with the lights out, and when an intruder looms up in the shadows, you roll for your gun and plug the guy between the eyes. Can't deny it, it did sound like a hoot, but as Mom used to say, it's always fun till somebody gets their eye poked out.

It is hard to explain to non-gun-owners the sensation of packing heat. Never mind that all ten of the bullets I had fired at the gun shop's range went wide of the target. Driving back home, it was enough to know that a theoretically mortal threat lay in the bag on my passenger seat. Having a gun close to you—or better, in your hand—confers the feeling of a superpower. And if that gun is concealed, it's a superpower that no one even knows you have, which is almost certainly the best kind of superpower there is. That first day I felt drunk with strength—intoxicated in a way you shouldn't be if you're operating heavy machinery, but that is apparently A-OK if you're handling a weapon.

I have to say, I didn't *like* that feeling of power. Or rather, there were twinges of guilt that went with it. After all, I'm a big supporter of gun control, and in a perfect world you wouldn't sell every kind of firearm to just anybody—and certainly not to somebody like me, who hadn't received the tiniest bit of instruction about the revolver I'd just bought.

To be honest, I'd hoped to get a quick lesson about my new plaything, but Sandy didn't have time that day. And after the fact, I decided that wasn't so bad. If I wanted the real American experience, instruction would just get in the way, since most of our countrymen have no training at all for the weapons they sling. To get in the American groove, I should probably have stored my revolver on a bookshelf, or in a child's toy basket. Loaded would be best, and altogether ready to fire. After all, if ever there's an intruder (or, say, a houseguest returning late), you don't want to be caught futzing with the safety.

In France, the experience is different. If you want to get a handgun here, there's really just one recommended course of action: forget it. They put you through a maze of required trainings, applications, waiting periods, and even letters of recommendation from the head of your local shooting club.

For that reason, I have never acquired a gun in France. But that didn't stop me from going for the kind of lesson I'd failed to get in the States. It's never too late to learn.

It's not easy to find a shooting range in Paris. In my neighborhood, with its 13 bakeries, 11 pharmacies, 7 fruit-and-vegetable shops, 6 wine merchants, and 5 shoe-repair places, there are precisely zero gun shops. In the entire capital, there are really only a handful of places where you're allowed to shoot firearms, and most require a trek across town.

That said, the rather austere Tir 1000 is within striking distance of the rue Bobillot, so that's where I went.

Tir 1000 is built like a bunker. Nondescript on the outside, where it snuggles against a frozen foods store, the inside consists of a reception area and waiting room, not unlike what I would find at Docteur Pédron's office when I go for a checkup. Pédron's walls are adorned with pictures of the Alps, whereas Tir 1000 prefers large blowups from various TV shows and movies—a sexy Dianna Rigg from *The Avengers* pointing her Beretta at the camera, Daniel Craig with a Bond-approved Walther PPK at his side, and that scene from *Pulp Fiction* where John Travolta and Samuel Jackson aim their Star Super B's at Marvin. There's even reading material in the waiting room of Tir 1000, though instead of well-thumbed health magazines, these were back issues of a publication called *Cibles* (Targets), the covers of which displayed various handguns. All in all, it left me with the impression that if anything went wrong at Tir 1000, you might find yourself transported to Docteur Pédron's on a stretcher, and hardly notice the difference.

Like many items of interest in Paris—say, the catacombs, the Metro, the sewers—the main part of Tir 1000 lies deep underground, at the bottom of a spiral stairway that leads to the shooting galleries. My class was taught by Hervé, a roly-poly ex-military fellow who enjoyed alternating barked orders with deadpan irony. For the next 45 minutes, two other novitiates and I squeezed our triggers through positions A, B, and C, learning how to blow away paper targets hanging twelve feet in front of us.

It's hard to make chit-chat while firing a 9 millimeter Glock, especially with those pesky earmuffs on, but when we finished I mentioned to Hervé how surprised I was that a gun shop and shooting gallery could make a go of it in Paris.

He scoffed. "We have 1500 members. This is my tenth class of the day. Everybody in Paris wants to be John Wick."

I don't know why this saddened me. Somehow I'd hoped Paris would be better than that. But maybe people are the same everywhere, eager to do each other in, if only they're given the chance.

I rolled up my target, brought it home, and hung it up on my bedroom wall.

Back to Checkov's gun, and all that.

The guy in the rue Bobillot was scrambling from the front seat of the black Mercedes convertible, after grabbing what he needed in the glovebox. Those poor city workers didn't see it coming. The boss was puffing on his cigarette, the thin one and the pudgy one were chuckling over another joke, and the two others still stared at their phone, too bored even to scroll.

That's when the burly, unshaven guy bounded before them and brandished his weapon.

It was a piece of paper—some kind of form. The skinny guy looked it over, shrugged, and handed it to his pudgy partner, who, in turn, passed it off the boss-man. The boss rubbed his bald head and frowned as he read it, then turned away to make a quick call—disappointingly not even on his radio, but just a cell phone. Then he handed the sheet back to the driver, sighed, and nodded at his underlings. They lifted one end of the yellow panel blocking the road and swiveled it to the side. The way was free. The driver hopped in, the engine revved, the tires squealed, and all returned to normal on the rue Bobillot.

What mysterious incantation did that paper hold? I'll never know for sure. But it demonstrated one incontrovertible truth. America is built around the myth of Shane, the lonely gunfighter. In France, however, the most powerful weapon is bureaucracy.

16
Wildlife

THERE'S A MOVIE ABOUT PARIS where a rat climbs the ladder of *haute cuisine*. Rémy has talent galore but no opposable thumbs, so he recruits a garbage boy to stir pots and sprinkle spices. Customers swoon, and by the time the credits roll, the bewhiskered protagonist with the ginormous schnozz has conquered the critics, whipping up dishes that would bring drool to the lips of Alain Ducasse. In one fell swoop Rémy lays to rest the idea that *rat* and *restaurant* should never be found in the same sentence.

All this to say that when Danielle called an emergency meeting about how rodents were taking over our building, I had to ask myself if life was imitating art. After all, there is a boulangerie on our ground floor, and all those *boules* and *baguettes* are baked on the premises. Could it be that a rat sporting a chef's toque had been rolling croissant dough on a marble countertop?

Alas, no. The activity had been detected deep in the cellar, where dark pellets were scattered fecally across the floor. Gnaw-marks had been spotted on the edge of a door.

When you've been living on your own for as long as I had been, it's odd what passes for entertainment. I wasn't so hungry for companionship that I was ready to cohabit with rodents, but there was something novel about this most recent event. It took me a moment to figure out why: it was the first major drama in our building association that Anne wasn't present for. How she used to love them!

At the meeting, it quickly became apparent that the members of our committee were appalled by the presence of rats in the cellar. But I didn't get why they were so shocked. Paris is the fourth most infested city in the world, with rats outnumbering Parisians three to one. It's not unusual to spot a long-tailed scavenger slinking next to you on the sidewalk (they prefer to creep by the wall), and in parks they loiter near benches, praying for bits of cheese to drop from lunchtime sandwiches. I don't recommend that anyone do a google search of the words "Paris," "rat," and "supermarket," but if you happened upon the results you'd have a pretty good idea—after wiping the sick from your lips—how much these creatures are part of the landscape here, just as much as checkered tablecloths, Bateaux Mouche and bad peanut butter.

Still, rat poop in our cellar was a bridge too far. To fully appreciate why, a little background is necessary.

Our building has suffered through many excremental afflictions over the years. There was *la dame du cinquième*, whose dog left deposits in the hallway—moist ones, as slippery as a banana peel, and hard to make out at the top of the stairs. After that was resolved, we faced the mystery series of human turds in the garbage can room. Cracking that case took a while. And then, for as long as I have lived here, there has been the problem of deteriorating plumbing, where waste lines eight stories tall occasionally burst forth with diarrheal fury.

I have chronicled these tribulations with the diligence of a medieval scribe, out of a sense of duty, but let's be honest: nobody takes pleasure in such events. Even I recognize there's no honor in telling tales about *merde*. It's a cheap laugh, and you feel dirty afterward. The wisecracks spill out on their own—quips about someone *launching a torpedo* or *cooking a burrito*—and right away you don't feel good about your work.

All this to say that we've faced bigger poop problems than this, and the presence of droppings the size of cupcake sprinkles felt belittling, as if fate were just rubbing our nose in it.

Second, there's the fact that our basement is a deeply scary place. Although the building dates from the 1930s, the cellar seems somehow more ancient, reaching back to the Middle Ages, at least. Architecturally, it occupies an unusual middle space, part dungeon, part House of Usher. In that low-ceilinged cavern, a narrow passageway leads spinelike down a center aisle, ribs of storage pens branching off. Each stall is framed in rough timbers, walled with broad planks, and sealed with lopsided doors bearing padlocks as large as a bear's paw. As a final flourish, our subterranean labyrinth was at some point wired for electricity, leaving a handful of bare bulbs connected to timer switches designed to plunge you into black when you reach the deepest recess. The only saving grace of the ensuing darkness is that you can't see why the floor is so sticky, and why that stickiness smells of decomposition.

My storage stall is one of the most distant, which means I visit it infrequently and with great reluctance. In principle, people use their stall as a kind of swing space for possessions they need only occasionally. But for me, taking an object down to the basement is a form of permanent banishment. A dismantled shelving unit I no longer need lives down there, along with a bicycle that will never again see the light of day. I believe the wadded mass in the corner is all that remains of curtains Anne had me take down there some twenty years ago. Next to it sits a bag of old clothing, turned down by the local charity. In short, I use the cellar the way Egyptians used pyramids—a place to stash things that you once loved and can't quite part with, even though you're damn sure you never want to see them again.

At the building committee meeting, we discussed what measures we should take. One option—which I consider our go-to plan for almost everything—was non-intervention. Yes, the rats had taken over the basement, but maybe that would be enough. We could sit on our hands, because they wouldn't demand anything more. This kind of politics of accommodation has an uneven past in European history, but you never know. Rats aren't Hitler, or even Putin. Any further annexation was almost certain to be gradual. There was debate about whether rats could climb stairs, but operating the elevator seemed clearly out of reach, which meant it would be some time before they made it to the upper floors—where, coincidentally, all the members of the building committee happen to reside.

"Good grief," Madeleine said, shaking her head. "Somebody should write a book about this place."

Then, as so often happens, a vague and annoying sense of duty settled upon us, and we resigned ourselves to taking action. *Les rats* needed to go.

A non-trivial portion of the French economy is dedicated to the eradication of unwanted house guests. *Désinsectisation*, for example, is the practice of spraying for roaches, ants, and other creeping entities. A team dedicated to *dépigeonisation* will oust everyone's favorite bird from your window ledges and eaves. Some joke that France could do with a bit of *désaméricanisation*, and when that happens, I'll be hitting the road. In this particular case, we required a service specializing in the science of *dératisation*.

But here's the kicker: *we already had one.*

Twice a year a man in blue coveralls comes through the building to check for mice and rats, a group collectively known as *rongeurs*. In various parts of the cellar, the ratologist

places small serving stations of delectable poison, known as
mort-aux-rats, or "death to the rats!"—a revolutionary cry
that is written boldly across the cardboard dispensers—on
the assumption that the intended victims have not yet
gained the ability to read. Instead, the rats belly up to the
dispensers and gorge themselves on slow-acting poison, after
which they return home and die peacefully in their sleep. Or
some such.

At present, the question was whether our man-in-blue
had failed to replenish the supply of toxins, or if our situation was entirely different, and perhaps much worse? What
if they'd gotten used to it? It seemed possible—perhaps inev-
itable—that years of such treatments would give rise to a
super-strain of death-resistant rats. It might be that just such
a mutant population was now making its move on the rue
Bobillot.

Danielle and I were dispatched on a mission to find out.

Danielle is a slight woman in her mid-seventies. She keeps
her white hair coiffed in the shape and consistency of a
cumulus nimbus. Her shoes are typically light in color, and of
the sort I am tempted to call dainty. The only special equip-
ment she donned for our expedition was a periwinkle-blue
cardigan.

Me, I took things more seriously, pulling on my hik-
ing boots, and tucking the cuffs of my jeans into my socks.
Gloves seemed like a good idea. I also carried a flashlight,

in case a rat gnawed through the wiring at an inopportune moment, plunging us into darkness.

We reconnoitered at the basement door. Danielle looked me over and rolled her eyes.

"What?" I said.

She shook her head and snapped a button of her cardigan in a determined way. "*On y va,*" she announced. It was game time.

As is standard in horror films, the stairs to our cellar are dark, twisting, dark, steep, and dark. Always the gentleman, I allowed Danielle to pass before me.

I'm rarely a fan of descending into pitch black, but the descent is even more unsettling when the dark refuses to remain silent. Muffled noises sounded before us. A kind of shuffling, along with—could it be—actual voices?

Danielle punched the timer button with her fist, casting a pale halo of light over our immediate surroundings. To our right stood the steel door that led to the kitchen for the boulangerie upstairs. That's where the voices came from. The bakers were at work.

"Look!" she cried, pointing to tooth marks at the base of a wooden post. "There. And there!"

On we went, down the central aisle, the soles of my shoes smacking with stickiness. A weight filled my stomach. As the floor turned gummier and gummier, my Spidey-sense tingled. The whole thing smacked of a set-up, an ambush— specifically, a large-scale version of the very glue traps that we so often use on rodents, which they may now have redirected at *us*. Everyone knows how smart these animals can be, but such a ploy would represent a giant leap forward, signaling that the rats had mastered—I shuddered at the thought of it—*irony*.

With the help of the flashlight, we confirmed that the rat man had indeed come by. Packets of *mort-aux-rats* were tucked in corners and under doors, and most had been nibbled open, half of their contents gone.

And yet, at the same time, fresh droppings were visible here and there—clear evidence of survivors.

Danielle gave me a look of confusion. Suddenly, the idea of the super-strain no longer sounded so silly.

It was at this point that we made our discovery. Under the dim light of the overhead bulb, the white-gray of the sticky floor was marred by flecks and scratches that grew more concentrated in one of the alleyways. The pattern gradually narrowed, forming what could only be called a *trail*, one leading directly underneath the loose door of the last storage pen.

We exchanged another look, and Danielle's steely gaze turned distinctly unsettled. The planking on the door was too tightly fitted to make out much through the cracks, so she pounded on the wood to scare back whatever awaited. I yanked the door open. In the dimness inside, a large mass sat slumped—a lumpy hillock of white, as if the Pillsbury Dough Boy, locked in this dungeon, huddled before us.

Then something moved.

If I interrupt this little adventure at the *moment critique*, it's not from some crass desire to gin up suspense, but rather the noble goal of sparing the reader, for as long as possible, the triggering of his or her gag reflex. Rats affect people in ways that other rodents don't. As far as I'm aware, no one has yet made a horror film teeming with, say, hamsters, despite their family resemblance. Inexplicably, even gerbils are considered by some to be unrepulsive. Back home, in Minnesota, people actually ooh and ahh over the frolicking antics of squirrels, even though they're merely a long-haired version of their cousin.

No, the only thing that comes close to rats on the Disgust-o-Meter are their smaller relatives, mice.

Which are also plentiful in France. My earliest memory of mice in France—well before the arrival of Mickey at Disneyland Paris—dates back to the happy days when Anne and I were recently married, living a carefree and possession-less life in a city near the Pyrenees, at the start of our very first year in this country. Our apartment was on the second floor of a hundred-year-old building that remained unspoiled by the major innovations of the twentieth century. The lights sometimes worked, and the water ran, which met our basic needs. But one thing kept us up at night, and that was the sound of scuttling in the ceiling above our bed.

For a few days, we avoided bringing up the subject with one another, since mentioning a thing has a way of making it real. After all, maybe those noises were just the wind, or some wandering ghost whose toenails needed to be trimmed. But one evening after dinner a shriek sounded from the kitchen and a plate smashed. A mouse had run across Anne's foot. Over the next days we spotted others—including one that leered at me from a high ledge while I showered in the morning. They were growing bolder.

Some things cross all cultural boundaries—such as the non-responsiveness of landlords—and this left us to take matters into our own hands. Anne suggested that we get a cat, and when I pointed out that our lease didn't allow pets, her eyes thinned. "What exactly does that mean?" she said. And soon she had me convinced that if we allowed mice to live in our home without making any attempt to evict them, they were, by any reasonable definition, *pets*. Surely it would be preferable to have one large household animal than many small ones. Any court in the land would agree to that.

We called the cat *Assassin*, and she lived up to her name, all those years ago. I miss her still.

There are plenty of mice in Paris, too, despite the half million cats that call the city home. Not far from the rue Bobillot is one of the city's great green spaces, the *Parc Montsouris*, the name of which translates as Mouse Hill. A famous windmill used to grind grain there—attracting scads of rodents. Still, things change. These days, it's not so much field mice you find trotting past the playground at the *Parc Montsouris* as rats of the Norwegian Brown variety. Along the shore of the pond in this park there are signs every fifty feet telling people not to feed the wildlife, and every ten feet there's someone doing just that, tossing out bits of bread or leaving a trail of pastry crumbs. If you're a rat, Montsouris isn't a bad place to reside.

Otherwise, though, you could live in the basement of our building, which had evidently also become a popular choice.

That's where, you'll recall, Danielle and I had just yanked open the door of the last storage stall. The flashlight swept across a lumpy white mass nearly five feet tall. They were sacks—large ones, bigger than pillows, piled like bags of cement at a construction site. White powder trickled from a recently nibbled corner.

What flashed through my mind was *The French Connection*. Right here, in the middle of the thirteenth arrondissement, I had uncovered, with the help of a pensioner in a periwinkle-blue cardigan, the world's largest heroin stash.

Or else flour.

The bakery in our building creaks into motion in the wee hours every morning, when two apprentices in their mid-twenties fire up the ovens. One by one, the mixing vats come alive, and giant dough hooks begin their wobbly spin—all part of the long process of churning out the batons of bread that France is famous for. In the beginning, though, a baguette starts its life a hundred and fifty miles away, on stalks of wheat grown in *la Beauce*, the region known as the breadbasket of the country. Not far outside of Paris—but no longer at the windmill of the *Parc Montsouris*—millers turn the grain into flour, filling 25-kilo sacks, some which are delivered weekly to a basement stall in our cellar on the rue Bobillot. Throughout the week, bakers trudge back and forth, dragging sacks across the uneven floor, flour trickling from the ruptured seams, coating the cement with a sickly white paste that sticks to your shoes.

What, you find yourself wondering, has burrowed into those bags? How long would the creatures have stayed? And how many cupcake sprinkles would they have left behind?

The image that sprang to mind was the glass case in the bakery shop upstairs containing trays of *pains au chocolat*— the famous chocolate croissants, golden brown on the outside, almost fudgelike in the middle.

There's a shop not too far away called Hygiène Premium. It specializes in the removal of vermin of all shapes and sizes, starting with ants, and culminating just before in-laws. The display window reminds me of those restaurants in certain foreign countries where tourists can choose their meal by pointing at wax replicas of available dishes. At Hygiène Premium, the figures on display are not made out of wax, but are instead creatures of the taxidermied sort. On one of the shelves in the window, a horde of cockroaches masses in a state of permanent alertness, as though the troops are ready to break formation and scatter when a kitchen light goes on. A catlike animal I'm tempted to call a marmot climbs a yellow pole toward the ceiling. And an even larger mammal with buck teeth—are beavers possibly a problem in the capital?—cocks his head with curiosity from the corner.

But my favorites are the rats, shown in poses I don't usually associate with their natural world. One miniature diorama displays four of them seated at a poker table, laying their wagers. One of them holds three cards in his paw— all aces—and has just discarded the two of diamonds. The player across from him holds a four of diamonds, and he looks huffy, as though he needed the other rat's card to complete his flush. You have the vague sense that a fight might break out. In another scene, two rats—one rather flea-bitten— have donned boxing gloves and face off in a ramshackle ring. To the right, between cans of insecticide, a Charles Dickens rat stands erect with a top hat and cane, a red velvet topcoat draping down to his thighs. And on the top shelf, presumably to shield the scene from the eyes of children, two rats appear to be engaged in a form of lovemaking sometimes referred to among humans as a 69—although they aren't quite limber enough to pull it off, so it's more like a 66 or 67.

No matter how you slice it, Hygiène Premium conveys the sense of a place that knows its pests, a suspicion confirmed just as soon as I pushed through the door. The man who leapt up from behind the counter, where he'd been sneaking a sandwich, was in his mid-thirties. He had close-cropped hair and a sturdy nose, along with the kind of athletic energy you want in a foot-soldier. His nametag identified him as Sacha.

I apologized for interrupting his lunch, but he batted away my concern. "Always here," he said. "Always open."

It's important when dealing with professionals to demonstrate your own authority, so I introduced myself as a member of our building committee. This has the power of a press pass in journalism: people suddenly take you seriously. As I related our tale, Sacha leaned in, and his eyes went small. He was no longer behind the dusty counter in Hygiène Premium, but deep in the bowels of a cellar on the rue Bobillot. This was a man who had not just lived *in* cellars, but *for* them. Yes, he knew just what the stalls were like, along with the timed lights that would plunge you into darkness. The presence of a bakery in the building made him cackle with delight—a new and interesting wrinkle to the challenge.

As I explained where the sacks of flour were kept, he cut me off, his two hands rising before him as though to frame the scene.

"So, they *drag* the sacks across the floor," he muses. "Right? And the flour trickles out."

"Exactly."

"So, tell me. Is the floor all cement?"

The question gave me pause, and I squinted to remember. There was a small tiled area over by the florist's storage, but also a rougher section next to the boilers. I remembered digging into it with my shoe at one point.

"Actually, there's a part that's just dirt, where the cement is crumbling."

Sacha's eyes lit up, and soon he explained why this was of interest. Rats can *burrow*.

Another scene sprang to mind that might be suitable for the Hygiène Premium display window. Next to the Charles Dickens rat there'd be room for a diorama of rodents enacting a scene from *The Great Escape*. They'd be digging tunnels with pint-sized trowels, concealing dirt in their trouser legs, avoiding the gaze of sentinels like me.

"Can you do something about it?" I said.

He shrugged. "We're good. But we're not magicians."

So that was that. We'd be living with these new neighbors forever. Eventually they'd widen their tunnels. Who knows? Maybe they'd lay down some HO track from a toy store, and build their own Metro to go from building to building. Soon they'd learn how to operate the elevator.

How would I break the news to the building committee? I trudged to the door, heavy with fate.

"Wait!" Sacha beckoned me back, wagging his finger. "There is a way."

Laying a sheet of paper next to his unfinished sandwich, he began drawing it out. First we'd chip away the crumbling floor, hauling out the debris in giant sacks. Then a chute through the window would deliver yards of sand and gravel to be spread and tamped. Once all that was done, we'd encase the entire floor under a cowl of cement.

It was nothing less than the Chernobylisation of our basement.

And that's what the building committee decided on. It would be a big project, and it would take a while—the kind of vast endeavor the Pharaohs might have tackled. But in the process, Sacha and Hygiène Premium would hoist us above the dross of daily melodrama. This was the real thing, what we all longed for—the kind of grand story everyone loves.

For now, though, the hubbub died down, and our building returned to quiet. I looked about the empty apartment. Nothing had changed. Not a chair had moved. And I had to wonder. It's like that tree in the forest. Does an epic tale even exist if there's no one there to hear you tell it?

17

The Parisite

VAMPIRISM IS SUCH AN UGLY WORD, heavy with creaking caskets, capes, fangs, and full moons. Those lonely souls get a bad rap for sucking blood, but what is it they're really after? To snuggle up, maybe. A bit of warmth. To feel the breath of life upon them once again.

Is that so bad?

For me it started, as so many things do, in a restaurant in Paris. I was seated in the back, alone at a table for two, pushing bits of food about my plate while I pondered what to do with my life, or what remained of it, which also felt like table scraps. People talk about all the wisdom and perspective that comes with age, but as far as I can tell, the main advantage to getting older is that you stop worrying about the "sell by" dates on foods at the grocery store. After all, if there's a better-than-even chance that I'll expire before the eggs do, why bother?

My musings were interrupted by the arrival of an ancient and heavyset man who limped up to the table next to me.

He plopped down on the bench seat, panting audibly as he recovered from the exertion of crossing the dining room. The charcoal gray suit he wore was rumpled and cut wide, in a style that harked back to some earlier age. From his ears, tufts of white hair sprouted, and ashen duffle bags sagged beneath his half-closed eyes. When the waiter announced the specials, he strained to hear, and when he reached for his glass of water, he sent it toppling. Then, in a final humiliation, his napkin slipped from his lap to the floor, and he couldn't bend far enough to retrieve it.

It was at this point that I found my own appetite returning. Not so much for the overcooked bits of chicken on my plate, but for the life seated at the next table.

My fellow diner wore a gold ring on his left hand—a wedding band, no doubt—although judging by appearances, it had been a long time since he'd undergone any sort of spousal inspection. His battered running shoes suggested foot problems, and the laces were tied loosely, in a way that allowed them to be slipped on and off without the hard reach. No, he'd arrived in this restaurant alone, and by the looks of things, he also lived alone, dressed alone, ate alone, slept alone. Every atom screamed deprivation. The universe was shrinking around this poor fellow, reducing him to one last pleasure in life, a decent lunch at an OK restaurant, just close enough to home that he could make it there without collapsing.

At the end, when the waiter cleared his plate, asking loudly if all had gone well, the fellow nodded.

"Oh yes," he said in French. "I'll be coming back soon."

He paid, and as he labored to his feet, his gaze caught mine, and he gave me one of those pinched smiles required by courtesy. In his eyes, a bleakness appeared. A hint of resignation or defeat. I smiled back—though I realized instantly that I shouldn't have. For there was nothing to smile about here. Far from it. Because all at once I understood, beyond the shadow of a doubt, the one thing that this man did not—namely, that he would *never* return to this restaurant, or any other. Call it second sight, a sixth sense, a vibe, an intuition. But there was no question about it. I had witnessed the last meal of a condemned man, one whose end was near—today, tomorrow, or the next day.

With more help from the waiter, the fellow made his way toward the front. Pausing at the counter, he spoke with the host, who pulled out a big book and flipped through the pages.

He was making a reservation.

I pushed aside my plate. The chicken was no longer necessary. There had been no transfer of vital fluids, but despite myself, I'd just lunched on another man's life. And it satisfied a strange appetite.

You see it in the movies all the time. A woman in a gown retires to her room. She opens the window to the night breeze, letting in the light of the full moon. In bed, she falls asleep, her head tipped back on the satin pillow. And out of nowhere, He appears, soundlessly approaching the pale neck, bending down, parting his lips, the fangs glinting...

Was that me spreading the wings of the cape? OK, not quite. I wasn't turning others into the undead. But I drew nourishment from their lives. It satisfied a hunger.

And it all had to do, somehow, with my current state of solitude.

Widowhood requires a ton of adjustments. Of course, there are the big things—the empty house, the lack of touch, the stillness—but it's the many details of everyday life that catch you off-guard. You lock yourself out one day, only to realize no one else has a key. You have a hankering for a certain dish, but the recipe disappeared along with your spouse. You shiver in bed from the flu, awash in sweat, wondering who will find your body and how long it will take, expecting your corpse to be half-eaten by the cats, only to remember that the cats, too, have moved on to the Great Litter Box in the Sky, so that nothing at all will be left, except perhaps a mummy in bedsheets awaiting the kids at Christmas.

In short, everything turns the crank of the self-pity machine. Living alone is like having a walkie-talkie when there's no one at the other end. You rattle off your message, crying "Over!"—only to learn, again and again, that it truly *is* over, and that no reply will be forthcoming.

My experience with the old man at the restaurant signaled a hunger for contact, which surprised me, given my longstanding discomfort regarding other human beings.

Now, I'm no card-carrying misanthrope, but that's only because misanthropes are unlikely to form an association issuing membership cards. Generally speaking, though, I prefer the *idea* of other people to the people themselves. I'll get invited to some party or other, and at first I'll look forward to it. While it exists only as an abstraction, I enjoy the idea of get-togethers. But as the date approaches, and I realize I'll be stuck chatting with an actual someone—or worse, multiple someones—I try to see if I can weasel out of it, which I usually can't. Having a fellow sufferer to accompany you to such events—especially if she is more socially gracious than the boor she's with—would make the event more tolerable. But since I have none, when the fated day arrives, I study the clouds overhead, wondering if, by sheer willpower, I might squeeze snow and sleet from them, or possibly a tornado, depending on the season—anything that would excuse my absence. I haven't yet set fire to my own residence, but don't think it hasn't crossed my mind.

In the end, I trudge off to the festive event like a man marching to the guillotine.

But even this situation was rare nowadays, because the usual stream of invitations had dried up. Turns out, when you lose a spouse, it's not just one person who disappears. It's the whole network that goes down. That's partly because so many events depend on pairing up, and your singleness throws things off balance. You introduce the problem of the odd number at the dinner table—meaning someone will be left without a partner in the musical chairs of conversation.

Moreover, it turned out some of our friends were secretly just Anne's. I'd been accepted as the cost of doing business, and that business was no longer necessary. To be honest, who could blame them? But even with the others, the dynamic had changed. People were used to having both of us there for dinner, and suddenly it was just me, the sidekick—Igor, pushing his peas around on the plate. I'd become what, in France, is called a *pique-assiette*, that is, a person who shows up for meals although he has nothing much to contribute. You're just mooching off your host—like a tape worm or a bedbug or a brother-in-law.

Thus, if it was human contact I hankered for, I would need fresh meat. Only problem is, new friends are hard to come by as you get older, especially if you're a misanthrope, and extra-especially if you live in the United State of America, at least in the Midwest.

In Minnesota, for example, it has become possible to live without encountering other human beings, mostly. In the normal course of life, people are a scarce commodity. In my neighborhood, for example, we are endowed with wide side-walks, but they are generally vacant except during dog-walk-ing hours, when dogless people like myself are routinely and blessedly ignored. Overall, Minnesotans are burdened with a great deal of space, which means that we are spread out as sparsely as chocolate chips in a Walmart cookie.

It wasn't always this way. When I was a kid, plenty of activities would throw you together with people you didn't know. One of my favorites was the Jolly Troll, a smorgasbord restaurant featuring banquet tables with metal chairs upholstered in yellow vinyl. You'd go through the buffet, elbow to elbow with people you'd never met, heaping your plate with scalloped potatoes and Swedish meatballs and cranberry fluff. Then you sat wherever there was space. Your conversations—and sometimes your food—spilled over to the people next to you, while animatronic trolls waved from the sidelines. You never made new friends at the Jolly Troll, but you caught glimpses of the inner lives of other families—how the parents treated each other, what the kids were allowed to do, how much the big ones picked on the little ones, and who got to run amok. That alone was as nourishing as the Jell-O salad.

Good luck finding a Jolly Troll these days. They closed down years ago because people preferred to sit by themselves in a booth at Wendy's, where they place their order for curly fries on a screen. The improvements of modern life have pretty much obliterated your chances of encountering another human these days. I haven't seen a bank teller in years, and instead manage my financial life online. At the Kwik Trip, I pump my own gas and tap to pay. The supermarket has recruited me to check myself out. And although

I could in theory speak to others by phone, I typically send text messages—even through it takes me longer to type them than to call. Of course, the personal touch of a handwritten letter was long ago replaced by emails, and these days most such communications—certainly those from administrators at my college, but also from certain friends—appear to have been generated by ChatGPT. As soon as they invent a sharp-bladed helmet allowing me to cut my own hair, I'll have no contact with anyone ever again.

Paris, though, is different. Why? Partly because so many of us are crammed into such a small space. But mostly, it's the variety, the great spread of rich and poor, foreign and local, urbanites and yokels. Life and death themselves traipse across this stage arm in arm, just as I'd seen in the case of my lunch companion two days earlier—that lonely old man who by now would be lying dead in his apartment, probably on his bed, the battered old running shoes still on his feet.

What I mean is that Paris offers up a little of everything. If you have an appetite for human beings, the City of Light is the Jolly Troll reborn, a smorgasbord of other people's lives.

Everyone knows the experience. You're sitting on the terrasse of a café on the Boulevard Saint-Germain, in a neighborhood so expensive, the only thing you can afford in a hundred-yard radius is the inch-deep thimble of coffee before you. But you're not there for the coffee, or the Gucci handbags, or the Hermès scarves. No, the absurd price you just paid to the snotty waiter was the cost of admission. You have a front-row seat to the spectacle of the city—the cars and buses, the masses belching forth from the Metro station, the shabbily dressed man trying to sell you a flower, women and men of multiple shapes and sizes, all of them on a mission to do something somewhere, and for each one, you find yourself conjuring up a sliver of their existence.

That's what it was like for me now. I drew nourishment from people I didn't know and had never met.

I didn't have to sit next to them in a restaurant to absorb their warmth. To the contrary, just walking down the street, brushing through the crowd, I'd catch a phrase, a gesture, see a scowl, sneer, or shrug, and somehow a whole life would appear before me, like a genie flowing from a lamp. My eyes would light upon a person, and I'd see the children they'd never had, the job they'd struggled for, the fraught relationship with their mother, the unpaid bill, the bread to pick up, the post office stop, the dog to walk, the socks to darn, the plans, the dreams, the disappointments.

Stopping in a bar for a beer, I sat at my table and closed my eyes, taking in the hum of voices, a long medley of half-heard, quarter-understood words and phrases. *I know, I know…how about over there…not at all the same…and he took the curve really fast…thanks…here you go…haven't seen her since…uh-huh, uh-huh….at the end of my rope…just a second…okay, I'll call you…* Every phrase sparked a story.

At a museum, an exhibit showed portraits of people against barren landscapes, sometimes on roads, or living in tents. There were women with skinny children, men with empty eyes, hands pressed to the brow. There, too, I sensed the rest of their lives, beyond the frame, their pasts and futures.

I turned to my companion to make a comment, forgetting for a moment that I had no companion, only to look down and meet the eyes of a schoolgirl in a pixie cut. There were thirty or forty of these kids running around, on a field trip. The girl smiled. She had a tooth missing on the top, a new one budding through the gum. How old was she? Ten? Eleven? Sixth grade, I figured. As she dashed away, I could see her studies at the university. She would drop out and start a business. Photography—or was it event planning? Then, an unhappy marriage, followed by a happy one, two kids, an apartment in the Yvelines, vacations in a cabin among the pine trees of the Landes region, her haircut changed, she grew thicker, her husband left, but then came back, a grandchild appeared from somewhere, followed by a hip replacement, and then, well, then...

With vampires it takes a stake through the heart. In olden times, they buried suspect people with a scythe placed over the neck, so if the dead attempted to rise, they'd lop off their own head. But me, I wasn't sucking anyone's blood. It's just that people are filled with an excess of life, and as they walk down the street, it trails after them like a whiff of perfume.

I returned to the restaurant for lunch the next week. The waiter gave me the same table as before. And as I inhaled the warmth, the clink of cutlery, the voices and laughter, I pondered this new existence of mine, in the Jolly Troll of Paris.

They say the senses compensate for one another. You lose your sight, but your ears perk up. You go deaf as a post, but suddenly you can read the bottom line of the eye chart. So, too, with people. You lose one, and the others grow in importance. It was the unknown population around me who mattered now. And like a safecracker who sands his fingertips to detect the clicks, I'd learned how to open people up, furtively, without their even knowing.

That's when the front door opened, and a heavyset man in a rumpled suit came in, old running shoes on his feet.

It was *him*. Somehow still alive.

And this time, he had a dog with him, and behind the dog, a wife. The waiter greeted them cheerily and escorted them to the table next to mine, where they settled in, chatting. The man glanced at me, paused with a hint of recognition, and gave me a pinched smile. Reaching for the water, his sleeve grazed the wine glass, which wobbled but did not fall.

I'd been wrong about it all.

And that's when I decided to stop living through the lives of others. It was time to start a life of my own.

PART THREE

The Beginning

Yes, Time holds the reins, enforcing its brutal dictatorship. And it spurs me onward, like an ox, with its double prod. "Move it, you ass! Sweat, slave! Get busy living, you wretch!"

— Charles Baudelaire

18

A Thing I Saw: Epiphany

WHILE TRUDGING HOME WITH GROCERIES, cutting through an empty side street toward the rue Bobillot, I asked myself what I should do with my life. It was one of those gray days in the capital, when you feel a lid has been clamped over the top of the city, leaving you to stew. What nagged at me was the futility of it all. When I was younger, I kicked the can of meaningfulness down the road, figuring it was all going to make sense later. And every time I caught up with the can, I'd just give it another whack. But at this point—verging on retirement, my family unmoored, and still no cat in my life—I found it unnerving to see that empty road still stretching out in front of me. Wasn't it supposed to lead somewhere, eventually, leaving me with the sense that I'd arrived? Or should I be trying a different direction?

I'd made it halfway down the street when I looked up and saw the man floating in front of a high brick wall.

Dressed all in blue, the guy was sinking quickly through the air—though not as fast as gravity would ordinarily demand. And he didn't tumble or thrash, the way I would have, if I were falling from the sky. Young and slender, with a bit of beard, he stood erect during the descent, with one hand calmly raised. He was still about forty feet up when I realized that the wall behind him was the backside of the perennially crumbling local church.

That's when the penny dropped. That pose. This place. A descent.

It was the second coming!

Probably at Sunday school or in sermons they prepare people for this sort of thing, but as a life-long miscreant, I was caught off-guard. What are you supposed to do in this situation? Avert your gaze? Or get out your phone and snap a selfie?

At first I was surprised he'd choose this street—barely more than an alley, really—for his return. The other side of the church would have been better, where he could descend onto the front steps before a cheering and awe-struck crowd, or at least in front of the guys who usually recline on those steps while sipping cans of beer. Or how about right in the center of town, where there's a honking big cathedral that's pretty much designed for stuff like this?

But upon reflection, it seemed right he'd choose a humble neighborhood like mine, with practically no one to witness him.

The hardhat struck me as excessively cautious, though I guess he hadn't had a lot of practice. By my calculation, this was just his second time.

Twenty feet away, he touched down on the asphalt, arms splayed for balance, bending to absorb the impact, since even the godhead is at risk of knee trouble later in life.

Then I saw the harness, and my new faith flickered.

He unbuckled himself from the cable. On the ground before him lay a few hammers in different sizes. He picked up a silver lunch box.

Turns out the guy was one of those acrobats the construction crews call a *cordiste*, a fellow who swings from the rooftops to inspect the hard-to-reach nooks, rappelling down the walls. They were doing repairs on the church.

And while this savior of masonry dug into his sandwich, I resumed the trek home, a new spring in my step. You go through the years, hoping to unwrap the gift of life to find out what's inside. But maybe it's an empty box. The surprise is simply that there is no surprise, and while that isn't much, it's better than no surprise at all.

19

Swipe Right

"It's time," Catherine scolded me in French. "Life is passing you by."

I made a vague gesture with my hand, half-twist, half-flick, designed to suggest agreement in a noncommittal way.

"Don't do that," she snapped.

"Do what?"

"*That.*" She gave a clownish flap of her hand. "I've seen it a thousand times. You want me to think it means *yes* when really it's *no.*"

I clenched my teeth. She could be so annoying.

"We have to send you out there," she said, using the verb *lancer*, which is also the word for launching rockets, those things that consume tremendous amounts of energy just to rise off the ground before they explode. "You need to meet someone."

Catherine is my oldest French friend, and she plays the role of the sister I never had—which is not to say that I never had a sister, because I did, just not one who truly sistered me. Catherine had known Anne since forever, but after grieving that long loss with the rest of us, she'd now turned her attention to bucking me up. Every now and then she'd stop by for a meal when coming through Paris en route to the champagne producer she worked for. A year earlier she'd dragged me off for a holiday weekend on the island of Groix, five miles off the Breton coast. We sloshed around that booger of land under icy rain for two and a half days. Somehow, it didn't do the trick.

Her campaign to get me dating smacked of France, but in a trite way. It played right into the cliché of Paris as a city of romance, a place where a thing called "love" happens in some sparkly way, where French men twirl their mustaches and make guttural chuckles in the direction of young women (or, if you're Maurice Chevalier, *leetle geerls*).

But, come to think of it, that wasn't so different from how Catherine had lived her own life. She'd motored through three husbands over the years, and was now on number four. The practice of monogamy in its serial form came naturally to her. Her mistake was thinking I'd become Frencher than I was.

I started the hand gesture again, but caught myself. "I'll think about it," I told her, knowing that I wouldn't think about it, and that I'd simply dodge the bullet by crossing the Atlantic.

"So," my pal David said, "we've got to get you online."

I'd barely returned to the States, and already this?

A week later it was my crazed friend, Humberto—who usually could be counted on to side with stewing and brooding—who told me the same damned thing.

It had turned into an international conspiracy.

Problem was, I was kind of rooting for them. What if it really *was* time?

The idea made me wince. I was dealing with a pack of emotions these days—loss, relief, sorrow, boredom, loneliness, fear—but there was really only one that counted. The Big Boy.

After all, guilt has been the defining impulse of my life, from the little things to the larger ones. It has always guided pretty much everything I do. If being a slacker didn't fill me with so much remorse, I wouldn't pry my eyes open every morning. Cheating on my taxes always sounds tempting, but who would I live with if I could no longer live with myself? Like most of the ways people get messed up, it all goes back to my childhood, to those days when my sister—the one who never sistered me—locked me up during games of cops and robbers. At some point, she didn't even have to drag me to that closet anymore. I knew I deserved to be in the slammer. Throw away that key!

But losing a spouse takes guilt to a whole new level. It's like that Magic Porridge Pot in the fairy tale—the more you take out, the more it fills up. After a while, I'd grown used to the routine, and the vague misery of it felt comfortable. I can't speak for others who have dealt with loss, but I know there's a huge range of reactions. Some people handle it pretty well, and others not. And in some cultures the surviving spouse—yes, usually the wife—is encouraged to hurl herself onto the funeral pyre after it's lit, since life is obviously not worth living anymore.

But now had come the idea of *moving on,* which was guilt's version of a supernova, blinding and vaporizing. When the other person isn't there to release you from your vows, it smacks of infidelity. And while I sometimes admire those who are invulnerable to the judgments of others, I rarely achieve that level of indifference myself. In this case, there were so many people I might be letting down—not just my in-laws and Anne's friends, but especially the kids. How do you tell them you're *moving on?* Are you supposed to get permission? I tallied up my emotions again, counting them off on my fingers: guilt, guilt, guilt, guilt, and guilt.

And then, as if that weren't bad enough, there was also the prospect of *dating*—a practice I'd largely avoided throughout my entire life. At this age, it would just turn into an exercise in humiliation.

After all, when you're over sixty years old, it's already plenty hard to avoid embarrassing yourself. The indignities of age pretty much have that covered. I'm at the point where I try not to look at myself in the mirror while I shave, which comes with its own risks. In every week's junk mail I'm harassed by the thugs at AARP. And if that weren't enough, assisted living communities have started sending me brochures. The worst is when I come across a form on the internet that requires my birthdate, and I have to watch the decades scroll by, generation by generation, as I make my way down to 1958. Thank God there are still a few years below mine when finally I get there. Not long ago I happened upon a form that required me to click through the years one by one, and by the time I finished, I'd aged even more.

So why bother? I found myself doing the math. If I could hold David and Humberto and Catherine at bay for another ten years or so, maybe an early death would solve the problem for me. If push came to shove, there was always the pyre option.

It was Humberto who finally wore me down—or rather, convinced me that miracles could occur. He'd been perennially lovelorn for as long as I'd known him, lurching from one disastrous relationship to another, the last one leaving him in a maelstrom of depression that nearly sucked him under. Three years ago, though, he met Clair—online—and everyone finally got to see what a happy Humberto looked like. I barely recognized the guy.

"Escoti," he said, employing his Cuban version of my name, "you do it like this." He showed me the two-page portrait of himself he'd composed for the dating platform. I read it without blinking. He'd provided a window into his soul, but a pretty stark one, with no colored glass or decorative curtains.

"The goal," he said, "isn't to attract. No! You need to scare away almost everyone!"

It made a perverse kind of sense. Scaring away everyone sounded pretty good.

"All you have to do," Humberto continued, "is describe who you really are."

Little did he know what a challenge that would be. Self-reflection is one of my least favorite activities, and one I have successfully dodged throughout most of my life. Consequently, the person called "Scott Carpenter" remains mostly a mystery to me. I sometimes notice his name on bills and tax statements, but my acquaintance with the person in question is scant. When mail arrives with that name on the envelope, I'm tempted to send it back, scrawling "No longer at this address," or else "Recipient unknown," or even, in bold capital letters, "DECEASED." At Starbucks, I give them *noms de plume* to scribble on my cup—things like Gunter, Ricardo, or Mack—identities that I'm trying on for size. Even my few efforts at therapy ended in disaster, the last guy cutting me free after five sessions. "Let's maybe try this again some other time," he said. He'd fired me.

Humberto gave me dating homework, and I went home to compose a two-page portrait of the person who answered to my name.

Humberto had used the gay platforms, and I hadn't geared up for that big a change in my life. So I counted on David to guide me to the right dating app. The one he recommended had adopted an insect theme. In this universe, we lonely souls were somehow cast in the role of honey bees. It came with a hexagonal honeycomb logo, and your list of matches was called the beeline.

It made me wonder if the developers actually knew anything about the species *apis mellifera*. After all, bees are famous for not doing much of anything in the line of dating. They reproduce through parthenogenesis, which means the females just squirt out some eggs whenever they have a hankering for kids—no penis required. The app had the good sense not to take the metaphor too far, which would have required them to brand all the men on the platform—perhaps too pointedly—as drones. No mention was made of that fact that only females have stingers, and they totally glossed over the anaphylactic shock thing.

Rather magnanimously, I let these inaccuracies go by.

When you feel virtually costumed in a honeybee suit, it takes you down a peg. On the other hand, there's something humbling about thousands of people humiliating themselves together. You're all in the same boat—or hive—so you might as well put up with it.

I then subjected myself to The Algorithm, which was based on a handful of criteria about who I was and what I was looking for. It is, in every way, the second worst method in the world for meeting other people—narrowly beating out what we used to do.

Unlike the platform Humberto had used, the bee site didn't allow for the two pages of soul-baring narrative he'd made me compose. It limited my life story to 300 characters, which is barely enough space to finish clearing your throat, so that in the end you compress your entire being into a statement not even as long as this sentence. Some people adopted a telegraphic style, while others crammed in arcane abbreviations. A few didn't understand there was a length limit at all, so their bios were lopped off mid-

They were, in short, my people—awkward in every way.

The question was, what to say about Paris? Those five little letters have a way of crowding out the other 295. One magic word, and the only thing people see anymore is a candlelit dinner on a Bateau Mouche, opera houses, and men who dress a whole lot better than I do. The word "Paris" ramps up expectations, and there's no way reality wins in that contest.

So I left it out.

I chatted dutifully within the honeycomb, reviewing my beeline with the kind of scrutiny that only a compound eye can provide. Most interactions lasted a full two messages, but a few went farther, and before I could weasel out of it, I'd agreed to the first date I'd been on in decades.

We shall leave to the mists of time and the conjuring powers of the imagination just how that encounter went. Suffice it to say that it did not lead to a sequel, which was also true of my second first date, and my third. What a relief!

"All they did is talk!" I told David. "We were together for an hour and a half, and I could tell you ever single thing about their life—where they've lived, what work they've done, how many pets they've had, and what the pets' names were. Whereas, they didn't ask a single thing about me!"

"I see," David said. He stroked his chin. "So, it seems they made every effort to tell you something about themselves. And you did not return the favor. Is that about the size of it?"

I closed my eyes and let the steam evacuate through my ears.

And then I *did* meet someone. Sort of. I mean, she was terribly nice. Dreadfully thoughtful. Unnervingly easy to be with. We went for a dinner or two. A movie. And then, one evening, before I went home, we kissed.

And it was...OK.

By "OK" I mean that it was not unpleasant. I think I'd hoped for more, but maybe I was greedy. I began to think that "OK" was maybe what the universe had in store for me. Maybe "OK" is what you get when you've crested the hill of your sixth decade. Maybe "OK" isn't so bad.

But then, why was I still poking about on the platform, chatting with other honeybees? There was one woman who worked in a museum, which seemed like a good fit, given how old and crusty I'd been feeling. But she didn't seem in any hurry to get together. There was another, whose profile pictured her with all five of her dogs, and though we chatted for a bit, I knew I couldn't deal with that level of competition. There was a lawyer whose secret passion was—ugh—Broadway musicals. And there'd been that redhead with a smirking grin, the one who was clever in her chats, a fizzing wit. That held promise, maybe? But she came and went, long silences spacing out our texts. We'd talked about maybe connecting after the holidays. But her interest felt half-hearted.

That's when I pushed the ejection button and left for Paris. Wanting to start afresh, I redid my 300-character bio in French. Instead of being a Minnesotan who often jetted off to Europe, I'd be the Paris resident who occasionally slummed in the US. We'd see what happened.

The weird thing about dating in France is that it doesn't really happen. I don't mean that French couples never form. Let's state the obvious: they do. But the crazy stuff between the first encounter and the Big Commitment unfolds differently.

To begin with, there's no word in French for the activity we're talking about here. In France, the bee-themed app was called *une application de dating*, where they just threw in the English word. Some French websites tell you how to conduct yourself during such outings, which they refer to rather awkwardly as *un date*. It seemed gratuitously trendy until I realized there wasn't a good alternative. I mean, in French you can say you've got a *rendez-vous* with someone, but that might just as well be with your doctor or dentist, even if you're not romantically involved with them. I thought back to French friends, and how they described this practice. Typically, when one of them met somebody new, they would report they were "seeing" the person. But even this word evoked a kind of seriousness, signaling that the relationship has congealed. Turns out there's nothing in the French lexicon to express the possible casualness associated with the American notion of a date.

What did that mean? Sometimes when a word is missing in a language, it's because they say things differently—the way Americans have "other fish to fry" while in France they have "other cats to whip." But sometimes the missing word reflects a hole in the culture, a gap you will fall through if you're not careful.

My own experience in this area was thin. The only person I'd almost gone out with in France was Joëlle, a young woman with whom I'd exchanged significant glances during our summer working together in Brittany. Over forty years ago.

And yet, wasn't France the country of courtliness, Paris the heart of romance?

Or maybe it was the opposite? After all, the greatest novel in the French language is basically an anti-dating manual. In *Madame Bovary*, young Emma approaches each new relationship with the swashbuckling visions of romance that she drew from novels, where ardor is always undying, absence always unbearable, and adultery always available. But each time she finds a new lover, the entanglement follows the same arc, racing from the thrill of transgression and frenzied trysts, to guilt and logistical problems, followed, inevitably, by lovemaking on a schedule, the cooling of passions, and, worst of all, boredom. Emma's lovers tire of all the playacting, so she lurches from one betrayal to the next, showing what happens when people's desires become untethered from reality, when they give way to endless dreaming. The novel illustrates Flaubert's three-word definition of life: *hope, then disappointment.*

But throughout the whole book, Emma never went on an actual "date." The concept simply didn't apply.

So I checked in with my expert on all things Frenchly romantic—my sister, which is to say Catherine. And she confirmed that dating in the American style was not much of a thing here. People often got to know each other through collective activities—the way she'd met Husband Number Three in a choral group in Auvergne. For a while, you went out that way—in the protective, mutual chaperoning of a cluster of friends who might all be wooing one another. By the time you got to one-on-one, it meant things were turning serious, and if they were serious, you'd damned well better not be swiping right on other people on some lousy app.

What this means is that romance in France is more of a light switch—on or off—whereas in the US, it's a dimmer. You see it in public displays of affection. In the States, it's possible for a couple to just walk hand in hand, whereas anyone who has traveled to Paris has witnessed the problem romance poses for public health. Couples smooch at bus stops. They grope each other on park benches. They seem to be pleasuring one another on the Metro. Part of you wants to scream *Get a room*, while the rest of you feels that pinch of jealousy. The same thing comes up in TV shows and movies, where people peel off clothing while engaging in dialogue so suggestive it would make innuendo blush.

Not the kind of environment designed for an aging kid from the Midwest. Still, it was time to soldier on. Reluctantly, I zipped myself back into my honeybee persona, checking out the local blossoms.

The French are famous for their banter, and they basically invented repartee. Chatting online with French women didn't quite reach the level of *The Marriage of Figaro* or *Dangerous Liaisons*, but it wasn't bad. As in the States, people started out cautiously, showing little more than the hem of their personality, revealing a bit more over time. But unlike in the US, when you mentioned the word "Paris," the chat didn't fill up with emojis of stars and hearts. After all, these women lived here. Paris was just the backdrop. If it meant anything at all, it was traffic jams and bad parking, high prices and smog. Paris was a thing to be dealt with.

But there was something else, too. Dating in French felt bewitching. Exotic. After all, if I'm honest—and believe me, I don't want to be—it turns out I've been as hoodwinked as everyone else by France. If I go all the way back, French has always been tied to romance for me. Despite my pooh-poohing of clichés and my swipes at corny illusions, the only reason I got interested in this crazy language in the first place was because of women. It goes way, way back. My seventh-grade French teacher was a bescarfed beauty. In high school I fell hard for a Belgian instructor named Chantal. There'd been Joëlle, to whom I'd made cow eyes that one summer. And in college? I only wish I could say I chose those French poetry classes because the subject was so intriguing.

In the end, I went out with Elise, whom I met, of all things, outside of the app. She was—of course—a teacher, one was willing to coach me through the brambles of my own hesitations. Although she worked in the suburbs, she lived in town. Dark-haired and earnest, she was frighteningly cultured. We had a couple meals in the safety of restaurants. We went to the theater. And then, one evening, after dessert, out of the blue, she kissed me.

It was the culmination of a lifetime of fantasy. In the instant of the kiss, a deck of French women flicked through my imagination. Finally, a female from this country—a *Parisian*, no less—had found me desirable. Or, let's be honest: tolerable. Exoticism blurred into eroticism. Who knew where this might lead?

Tiny problem was, I hadn't felt anything.

I liked Elise. She was fun. We had lots to talk about. But when I checked my pulse, nothing had changed. I wasn't even sure I had one.

Once again my finger inched toward the ejection button. Time to jump ship, head back. Maybe that's how I'd live, ping-ponging between France and the US. Or maybe I should set up shop somewhere in the middle. They say Greenland is nice.

What is meant by "the spark"? As far as I can tell, it's that *je ne sais quoi* about a person that locks you together. For bees, on those occasions when they don't go the parthenogenic route, it's all about pheromones. For birds it's the plumage that shakes things up. In the case of baboons, it's all about how red the butt is. Every species has something to get the heart going.

What I needed was a defibrillator.

I considered returning to the States. There was that woman with five dogs. The curator at the museum. The lawyer who adored—ugh—musicals.

Nah.

Maybe that wise-cracking redhead, if she ever resurfaced. But no, she was clearly not interested.

One evening I was sitting by the living room window, watching the world go by, when suddenly it hit me. "OK" was *not* good enough. Half-measures weren't worth it. Even a spark would not suffice.

What I wanted was full-on electrification *or nothing*.

And because electrification wasn't available—because I'd reached the age where life serves up its days lukewarm and spiceless—I decided to throw in that particular towel. I'd been living like a monk for years now anyway, so this would just be one more privation.

As I thought about this other future, free of entanglements, liberated from that dangerous emotion of hope, my whole body lightened, and I felt almost dizzy, as though the floor had fallen out beneath me, leaving me momentarily afloat.

I recognized the sensation. It was relief. The search was over. The future came into focus. If I wanted to, I could stay in my pajamas all day, shovel down ice cream straight from the carton. Maybe I'd cheat on my taxes, just for the hell of it.

And you know what else? I would get a cat.

20

Paris Lost and Found

GIVING UP ON DATING WAS the best thing I'd ever done. Life is so much simpler when you don't have to bend to another person's needs or rise to their expectations. How, you find yourself wondering, did shaving ever become a thing in civilization? What would happen to the social order if you stopped? Might as well give that a test. Laundry, too, seemed a bit ginned up, the magnates of Big Detergent having convinced us that clean socks are the linchpin of society. And it turns out you can make a pretty balanced diet out of apples, peanut butter, and potato chips—fruit, protein, and vegetables.

The apartment on the rue Bobillot used to feel ample for two people, or even for a few, back when the kids were here, but lately it was growing cramped for one. Still, I made it work, always keeping a clear path through the dirty clothes in the bedroom. And in the kitchen I could almost always scoot things aside so there was counter space for apple-slicing.

My only problem was the parrots. Somehow, I'd been going to bed later and later, which left me hoping to sleep most of the next day. To guard against daylight I'd burrow under the covers, or else shield my face with the kind of mask Batman might have worn if, like the animal he imitated, he didn't mind not seeing at all. But whenever morning struck, a kind of yattering would start up outside my bedroom window. In the Linden trees out on the square, a brood of small green parrots had set up shop, and like roosters they began their noisemaking at dawn.

These birds are a blight in the city. They used to be found in southern Spain, but over the years, they'd expanded their territory—overrunning Madrid, conquering Barcelona, and fluttering their way northward along the A6, until finally, one day, they reached Paris, where one of them happened upon the square outside my building and liked what he saw.

It made me consider returning to Tir 1000 for another shooting lesson with Hervé. And maybe making a purchase.

Thanks to the parrot alarm clock, I'd crawl out of bed, put on the coffee, and whip up one of my special breakfasts—a delicate concoction featuring raspberry jam on ruffled potato chips. (Yes, that's fruit *and* vegetables in a single meal, the very foundation of the food pyramid.)

After this repast, I sat on the couch and waited for something to happen. After all, this was Paris. There was bound to be a problem with rats somewhere. Maybe someone would start leaving turds again. If I could get a fixture to break in the bathroom, I could head over to the Bricorama hardware store, and see what kind of havoc might ensue.

But all was quiet. Even the building committee had pushed the pause button on meetings. Nothing was going wrong these days.

The living room window had always been more interesting than any TV screen, and I spent hours watching the spectacle of life march by. Lately, though, the program in my window lacked pizzazz. I found myself wishing there was a remote, so I could change the channel. I wasn't asking for much. Maybe another almost-gunfight. Perhaps a showdown with the Corsican insurance agent—the one who strummed his guitar at all hours. But the city was strangely placid. Even the crazy woman who stomped down the street everyday seemed to be on vacation.

One day a worker in a knit cap changed the ten-foot-tall theater posters in the Morris column on the square, hoisting them up the way you raise a sail on a boat. That was something. And every few days a truck stopped by to service the public toilet. Not exactly high drama.

My pulse quickened one afternoon when a firetruck stopped right below my window, and gold-helmeted firemen jumped out. They pulled the ladder off the top of the truck and stood around. Was our building on fire? Was I? I craned my neck out the window, looking up, left, and right. Sadly, no smoke anywhere. Fifteen minutes later, they loaded the ladder back on top, jumped into the truck, and left.

False alarm. Or else the wrong address.

I considered going out—by which I mean to destinations other than the grocery store and bakery. But the movie theaters seemed far away. Seventy feet beneath the street were the catacombs, and in the past, I'd gone spelunking down there. But now it felt like a hassle.

So, I settled into a routine: eat, sleep, wake to the squawking, sit around, run an errand, eat, sleep, and dream of shooting the damned parrots. It was the life of Riley.

Eventually it was time to return to the States, where I began to craft an American version of my routine. Frankly, there it was even better, because we'd reached the point in civilization where everything you desired could be delivered to your doorstep, almost faster than you could get there yourself. Need some toilet paper? Click on Amazon. Got a hankering for pizza? You know the number. Anytime I needed something, it turned out there was an app for that.

Then, one day, the bottom fell out of this rich existence.

A message had appeared on my phone. "Hope you had a great trip," it said. "Would love to reconnect if you're up for it."

I stared at those words for a long time.

They'd come from the mysterious redhead on the *application de dating*, the bee-themed platform that I'd sworn off. She was the one who'd dropped in and out of the chat, who clearly had better things to do, who'd postponed the coffee date we'd attempted, just before I'd scurried off to Paris.

And now, two months later, here she was, contacting me out of the blue.

Every word in that message made the warning siren in my head scream. The very first one was *hope*—and we all know where that leads. Then came a pronoun referring to *me*. There was mention of *reconnecting*—which made me wonder if we'd actually made a connection to begin with.

But worst of all was the sudden and unexplained emergence of the word *love*. What the hell was that doing there? Sure, she'd couched it in a casual way, but there were so many better phrasings—things like, *It would be great to…I'd be happy to…Would you like to…?* But no, she had to go and say that she'd *love* to reconnect.

Thank goodness the last part of her message gave me an easy out. Because no, I was *not* "up for it." To the contrary, I had waved the white flag and surrendered to the enemy. I planned to spend my remaining years in a prison camp for old farts, sitting on a bench and whittling twigs into toothpicks.

A great battle ensued. No, I don't mean with Bonnie—that was the name of the impertinent creature who had reached out to me—but with myself.

Let me explain. Over the years I have come to recognize the presence of another me in me. Often, it sleeps, allowing me to conduct my affairs in a reasonable, rational way. But at the most inopportune times, the other being wakes. For example, I may have a deadline looming—one for which I have promised to complete a task, and where my failure to do so will have dire consequences for my future. The chore before me is eminently feasible, well within my powers, and yet the closer the date approaches, the less able I am to complete it—or, to be perfectly honest, start it. My entire body vibrates with urgency as the deadline approaches. I can practically see the hands on the clock turn. I order myself to sit at the desk and take action. But the other being within me has put on the brakes. Even guilt can't push me forward. Like a man handcuffed to a time bomb, I watch the minutes count down, then the seconds, and then it's too late.

The same thing happened this time, but in reverse. That is, I knew I was done with dating. That decision was signed and sealed. To make good on this commitment to myself, I only needed to do one thing, which was, conveniently, *nothing at all*. No action was required—or rather, what was required was the absence of action, which was typically my favorite state, especially these days.

How, then, to explain the activity of my hands? These strange, crab-like appendages moved as if according to their own desires. It was *him*. The other me. He was stirring. A great test of wills began, and I fought mightily, struggling to hold him back. But in the end, he won. My eyes watched helplessly as his thumbs typed out a reply.

"Sure," the thumbs said. "It would be great to get together. What's your schedule like?"

And just like that, I'd given dating a second chance.

One of the advantages of the internet is that geography—or at least distance—no longer matters. Let's say you're an aficionado of sixteenth-century Italian puppets. There are maybe a dozen others around the world with similar levels of interest and expertise in the topic. Years ago, all of you would have remained unknown to the other twelve, and you'd have pursued your passion in utter solitude. Thanks to the internet, you are now bound together. With a few clicks, you have formed an association. Who knows? Perhaps you have even attracted acolytes. You have *found* one another in the same virtual space.

Something similar happens for people with rare diseases, who can finally form a community despite living in different corners of the globe. It also makes organ donations easier, and it brings the DMV right into your living room.

The same can be said of the online version of dating. These days, you no longer have to hope that the girl next door will be both interesting and interested, because the net you cast is not just any net—it's the internet. Your soul mate may hail from Seoul, your paramour from Paraguay. There are no boundaries or borders. You have the entire world at your fingertips.

It was thus a disappointment to discover, during our text exchanges, that Bonnie didn't live in Denver or Denmark. She was down the street, within walking distance of my condo. That meant that after things didn't work out, we'd end up bumping into each other all the time at the grocery store or the dry cleaner's. Probably I'd have to stop shopping altogether. Or move.

Still, it was too late now, and after a few starts and stops, a couple reschedulings, we met. It happened in January at a coffee shop. I entered with the sense of relief that soldiers reportedly feel when they finally get to the front: you're done with all that waiting. In an hour, at most two, I could scratch this off my list and shut down the dating thing for good.

Inside the door, I stomped the snow from my shoes, took off my gloves. At the counter, a woman turned. Her cheeks dimpled with a smile.

It was her. She rose and greeted me. During the awkward introductions, she left pauses, actually listening to my halting replies. After I finished speaking, she spoke. And then I spoke again. It had many of the earmarks of a conversation.

All at once I suspected this wasn't going to be as simple as I'd imagined.

We sat for a long time, easing into topics and cushioning them with pleasantries. Soon we moved on to background and unpleasantries. No, Bonnie hadn't flaked out during those early exchanges, when she'd gone quiet for long stretches. Instead, she was grieving the loss of a close friend and was struggling to claw her way back to the routines of life.

Following David's advice, I shared an inch of myself. Talked about the kids. Told her about Anne.

Turned out, Bonnie had lost a mate, too. We compared notes and generally agreed that it sucks.

Then, somehow, we turned the corner on the serious topics. A joke surfaced, followed by a quip. That winning smile flashed again. She poked a bit of fun at me. The ambiance was oddly untroubled. And by the end of ninety minutes we had each cracked open the door, letting in a sliver of light.

I like to pretend that I am a unique creature, that I pilot my own way through life. At the same time, I know that this is an illusion, and we are all the playthings of genes and hormones. It's thus no surprise that I am in some respects similar to other individuals of the male persuasion, which is to say profoundly out of touch with those things referred to as feelings. Back during Anne's illness, my therapist (not the one who fired me) once asked how the responsibility of caregiving felt *in my body*, and I found the question baffling. I mean, yes, I guess I have a body, and presumably that's where feelings live. But was I supposed to be able to *feel* the feeling, the way you feel an ache in the knee or a sore throat? Phrenologists used to think a bump on the skull represented unhappiness or generosity. Was that what she meant?

I thought about it for two weeks, and at our next therapy session I was giddy with excitement, because I'd come up with an answer. "Heavy!" I told her. "It feels heavy."

I was proud of myself.

My first encounter with Bonnie had left me with the same riddle. What was that sensation in my gut? I was pretty sure it wasn't gastro-intestinal. As I puzzled through this problem, I found myself replaying our date in my mind, sometimes seeing it from different camera angles. There they were, two people in a café, one of them attractive. I could hear their exchange, almost as if I were eavesdropping on it.

The conversation had been both easy and guarded. On the one hand, I'd laid out my cards as frankly as possible, and I was pretty sure Bonnie had done the same. And yet, I'd also sensed a hint of caution. As they say, once burned, twice shy, and thanks to the dating game, I was like one of those victims in a burn unit, gauzed up from head to toe. From what I'd gleaned, Bonnie had been scalded a few times as well.

We went out again, on a second date, and the unnamable emotion inside me kept growing. I attempted to identify it. No, it was not just caution. Something bigger. But I couldn't make out the features.

Then, to make matters worse, another thought hit me. What about *her*? Wasn't it possible that Bonnie had feelings, too? The whole thing was turning complicated.

One evening we were stumbling along a snow-encrusted sidewalk as we passed an unusual building. It was the local curling club—that place where people with brooms buff the ice in a cold-weather version of shuffleboard.

Bonnie let fly with a quip about curlers, how they're always bad-mouthing their arch-enemies—the bowling leagues.

It was almost nothing. Just a little zinger. But it had some magical combination of speed and snarkiness and knowledge of the human soul, some *je ne sais quoi* that sent an electric current through me. I halted and stared. It had happened. I had felt myself feel something, and that something had to do with the blood coursing through my veins, the pump that makes it all happen. I'd been defibrillated.

All at once I recognized the emotion—that feeling I'd been desperate to identify. It had burst to the surface. And it had a name. I could almost see the four little letters that spelled it.

Fear.

Yes, that was it. The scaredy-cat was back in full force.

"What's the matter?" Bonnie said.

"Say what?"

"You look different."

She had this way of detecting things in me almost before I did.

I tried to whistle casually as we continued down the street, the way you might if Hannibal Lecter were holding your hand—by which I mean, of course, a rather *cute* Hannibal Lecter, one with a great sense of humor and other terrific qualities.

But Hannibal Lecter, nevertheless.

I once had the opportunity to climb to the top of one of those off-shore wind turbines. It's mostly humdrum. You go inside the giant stem of the thing and start clambering up the metal rungs, reaching a new platform every fifteen or twenty feet. When you look down, all you can see is the new floor a couple yards below you, so at any given moment, you're stuck in a small cylindrical room.

But then you reach the hub, and you pop out. They've opened up the cowl, and suddenly you're on top of the world with the wind howling, and you're not tethered to a thing. Waves crash mutely below. The coast with its tiny houses and roads stretches forever, and you're pretty sure you can see the curvature of the earth. You hang on tight, because one slip, and you're toast.

That's how our relationship was going. It was exhilarating up there, but I kept expecting to slip. Who knew what form it would take? Maybe she'd reveal she was a Branch Davidian. Or that her great passion was—ugh—Broadway musicals. Maybe I'd run out of charming things to say—I only had three or four to begin with—and she'd figure out what a mess I was.

But weeks had gone by, and the view was still tremendous. I'd grown used to the wind. And neither of us had yet fallen to our death.

"Say," I said one day, as casually as possible, "what's your opinion of…Paris?"

"Paris?" she shrugged. "Fine, I guess."

Fine? I squinted at her. Nobody in the world had ever given that assessment of the City of Light. *Fine*? I was losing my footing.

She turned and looked me straight in the eye. "OK, so here's the thing," she said. "I don't want to burst your bubble.

I know you spend a lot of time there. The truth is, I've been a couple of times, and I didn't think much of it."

She rattled off her reasons, something about a bad hotel, the lines at the museums, some other stuff—but the fact is, I'd stopped listening.

"You OK?" she said.

And I was OK. In fact, I was back on top of the world. A great wave of warmth had just rolled through my chest.

Little did she know, but "fine" was the perfect answer. Bonnie had seen the glitz of Paris, its self-promotion, the bit of leg it shows to tourists, all the parts that smack of cons and clichés. And she'd had the good sense not to like it.

Now all I had to do was talk her into giving the city a second chance.

There was still the guilt to be dealt with. Aside from secret consultations with Humberto and David, I hadn't breathed a word to anyone about my dating—much less the existence of a person named Bonnie.

There were only two people in the world whose judgment mattered.

I pecked out an email to the kids, Paul and Muriel. I re-read it. Re-re-read it. Then I hit send and waited.

Minutes passed. Hours. My stomach hurt. I began to second-guess myself. Maybe I should have worded it differently. Maybe it was too soon. Maybe it would always be too soon.

And finally the replies arrived. They were happy for me. "I thought it might be good for you to date," Muriel said. "But I didn't think I should be the one to bring it up."

They looked forward to meeting her.

And I took my first breath in hours.

Two months later, when I had to return to France, an idea was born, and before the censor in my head could beat it to death, I asked Bonnie to join me. Against her better judgment, she said yes. And before I knew what was happening, I had introduced her to the rue Bobillot, to Madame Estevès, to Danielle and Cyril. Together we visited the *local poubelles*, where the turds had appeared. Next was the cellar of rats. We went to the park and watched kids wipe out on the playground. Then it was time for the movie theaters.

And as we went through the city, I pointed out landmarks. There was the public toilet I'd watched them build. Over yonder was the Bricorama hardware store. Down that ravine you'd find the way to sneak into the catacombs. Here was the spot where prostitutes slunk out after dark. On the ground floor of my building, the Corsican insurance agent played the same folksong on his guitar all day long, falling apart at a tough chord progression, and then starting over. Again and again and again.

Wasn't it all great?

And somehow, against all odds, she *liked* it.

I'd spent years picking apart the romantic image of Paris. I'd dismantled the Eiffel Tower, shot out the lights on the Champs Élysées, drilled holes in the hulls of the Bateaux Mouche. And yet, here I was, afflicted with the strangest and rarest and most wonderful of feelings—one that I could finally identify in my body. It was lightness and warmth and energy.

The regime of dirty laundry and apple slices was over, and I was back to shaving on a regular basis. I wasn't discarding the past. That would always be there. But I'd found an opening to a future.

Outside the apartment, in the Linden trees on the square, the green parrots engaged in their daily riots, squawking and swooping, chattering in their high-pitched way.

"They started in Spain," I explained to Bonnie, proud that even these tiny details about Paris were within my command. I regaled her with the tale, how these flocks of birds had expanded their territory, generation after generation, making their way over the Pyrenees, finally migrating to Narbonne before a new batch broke away to make another great push northward, through Toulouse, then Lyon, their small wings bearing them over the wheat fields of *la Beauce*, until finally they reached the Paris basin, and—

"It says here they came through Charles-de-Gaulle." She was looking at her phone.

I chuckled. "Well, no, because that's north of the city, you see. They wouldn't have flown—"

"What I mean is, they were pets. Shipped to the airport. And then they escaped. That's how they got to Paris."

Her phone was in my face. There it was, in black and white.

She wore a self-satisfied smirk and began to chuckle.

"Well," I told her, "I don't think it's *that* funny." But my protestations just aggravated her snorts.

There are lots of theories above love. Plato cooked up the idea of each of us having an *other half*. Freud had that cockamamie notion about mothers. But in the end, doesn't life's most powerful emotion come down to this—to having one person in the universe who's close enough and sharp enough to call you on your shit?

That's what I'd been doing for Paris over the years— catching it with its makeup off. And now Bonnie was willing to do the same for me. Indeed, she embraced this new responsibility with gusto.

That was fine. I knew how to bide my time. And when the opportunity arose, I would be sure to return the favor.

A Note About the Text

The events recounted in this book largely took place between 2018 and 2022, aside from dips into the past (as in most of chapter one), which I have attempted to signal clearly. As is common in this kind of writing, I've changed a few names, cheated in some dialogues (where my failing memory didn't recall them verbatim), and taken other small liberties generally afforded the genre. For example, the order of the chapters doesn't always reflect the order of events. How could it? Since some pieces spring back and forth in time, it was a challenge to figure out where to put them. For this, and for any other shortcomings, the Muse—that great scapegoat of writers—is entirely to blame.

Acknowledgments

In this kind of memoir, it's hard to know whom to thank—or rather, where to stop. For starters, there wouldn't be any story at all if life hadn't smacked me down nearly a dozen years ago. And how bleak it would still be without the stroke of luck that helped me turn the corner. In some odd way, I couldn't have written this book without Fate making me its plaything. So…thank you, Fate. I guess.

More to the point, this book is inextricable from the events it describes. In a very real way it owes its existence to the many people who supported me during the years in question. That list starts with my kids, Paul and Muriel, and I can only hope I supported them half as much as they did me. Then comes the vast network of family and friends, including Tim, Gina, Kathy, Kelly, David, Dana, Mike, Laura, Lucie, Sarah, Barb, Kate, Nancy, Tom, Uli, Anne #2, Jenny (and the crew at Breck Home), the Cricket Bat Book Club, and a score of others, including my mom, an indomitable spirit who is my inspiration for aging well.

Then there's the writing part. The book would not have materialized without the encouragement of Larry Habegger and James O'Reilly, my editors and champions at Travelers' Tales. They're simply the best. Eric Vrooman helped with his expert reading. My agent, Victoria Skurnick, continues to chart my course through the high seas of publishing, where I would otherwise sink like a stone. Kim Nelson's wonderful cover captures the spirit of the story. And where would this project be without the presence, participation, savvy and love of Bonnie Harris? Absolutely nowhere, that's where.

Thanks, too, to Carleton College, which has supported (tolerated?) this and other pivots in my professional life, entrusting me with hundreds of students over the years. Those students have taught me a great deal—especially as they puzzle through their experiences in the greatest of cities, the capital of both solitude and adventure that we have all come to know as Paris.

Book Club Guide for
Paris Lost and Found: A Memoir of Love

Here are a few questions that might be useful for readers as they discuss *Paris Lost and Found.*

QUESTIONS:

1. *Paris Lost and Found* is at times a tragic story, but it's also very funny. Why did the author choose to blend these different registers? What effect does it have?

2. At the beginning of the book, Anne has started her descent into dementia. What connections are there between memory (or the loss of memory) and the city of Paris?

3. The book is divided into three sections: "The End," "The Middle," "The Beginning." What do you make of this backwards structure?

4. What chapters taught you the most about life in Paris? And what chapters made you reflect on the strangeness of the United States?

5. Paris is usually presented as the city of youth and young love. The author's experience is now that of a "senior." How does age affect his experience of the City of Light?

6. This is a very character-driven memoir, and the book is populated with oddball locals. What is it about these people that makes them quintessentially French?

7. Sometimes the most touching encounters in the book are with people we meet once and never see again—such as the young woman with the lamp in chapter 10, "Adieu." What does that say about the author—or about Paris?

8. On page 106 the author writes that "Not knowing people somehow improves them." What does he mean by that? Do you agree with him?

9. Many chapters begin with a mundane event—getting on the Metro, sitting in a movie theater, paying bills—and evolve into much larger dramas. What does this tell us about the author's view of Paris, or his way of experiencing it?

10. The author writes about many topics in this book—thefts, the difficulty of communication, love, illness, death, rats, guns, turds, movies, dating, money... What binds these chapters together? Is the book a collection of disparate parts, or an integrated whole?

11. Toward the end of the book, the mood turns pretty low. Even if the writing remains bright, the author is in a very lonely state. Is that loneliness made easier by being in Paris, or does the city make it worse?

12. The last chapters of *Paris Lost and Found* deal with the tribulations (and terrors) of dating. What role does age play in this final section? What does this ending say about the nature of love?

13. Does travel have curative powers? What do your own experiences suggest in this respect?

14. What do you make of the title of the book? In what way is Paris "lost and found"?

15. How has *Paris Lost and Found* changed your view of Paris?

About the Author

Scott Dominic Carpenter teaches French literature and creative writing at Carleton College (MN) and is the author of *Theory of Remainders: A Novel* (named to Kirkus Reviews' *Best Books of 2013*), *This Jealous Earth: Stories* (2013), and *French Like Moi: A Midwesterner in Paris* (2020; a Midwest Independent Bookstore Bestseller). His credits include a Next Generation Indie Book Award, a Solas House Gold Award, a Mark Twain House Royal Nonesuch Award, Foreword Indies Book Award (finalist), the Paris American Library Book Award (honorable mention), and a "notable essay" listing in *Best American Essays*. His shorter work has appeared in a wide variety of venues, including *The Rumpus*, *Silk Road*, *South Dakota Review*, *Catapult*, *Ducts*, *Lowestoft Chronicle*, and various anthologies. His website is located at www.sdcarpenter.com.

Other Books by Scott Dominic Carpenter

French Like Moi: A Midwesterner in Paris. When Scott Carpenter moves from Minnesota to Paris, little does he suspect the dramas that await: Scheming neighbors, police denunciations, surly demonstrators, cooking disasters, medical mishaps—not to mention all those lectures about cheese! It turns out that nothing in the City of Light can be taken for granted, where even trips to the grocery store lead to adventure.

In *French Like Moi*, Carpenter guides us through the merry labyrinth of the everyday, one hilarious faux pas after another. Through it all, he keeps his eye on the central mystery of what makes the French French (and Midwesterners Midwestern). Winner of a Next Generation Indie Book Award, a Solas House Gold Award, a Mark Twain House Royal Nonesuch Award, and recognized for the Forward Indies Book Award (finalist), and the Paris American Library Book Award (honorable mention). ISBN: 978-1609521837

Theory of Remainders: A Novel. At fifty-two, psychiatrist Philip Adler is divorced, alone, and gutted of passion. When a funeral draws him back to his ex-wife's homeland of France, the trip reunites him with a trauma he has struggled to forget: the brutal death of his teenage daughter fifteen years earlier. Prodded by his former brother-in-law and stirred by the unspent embers of his marriage, he embarks on a mission to resolve lingering questions about this past, hoping to heal himself along the way. The search leads to a disturbed man who may hold more answers than anyone expects—if only Philip can hear what he's trying to say.

A suspenseful literary novel set in the lush backgrounds of Normandy, *Theory of Remainders* explores the secret ties between love, trauma, and language. It was named one of the Best Books of 2013 by Kirkus Reviews, and is currently being made into a major motion picture by T-Street Productions. ISBN: 978-0988904910

This Jealous Earth: Stories. A man puts his beloved pets to the knife; a family prepares for the Rapture; a woman in a department store slips a necklace into her purse. Whatever the situation, the characters in *This Jealous Earth* find themselves faced with moments of decision that will forever alter the course of their lives. Always moving and often touched with humor, Carpenter's stories examine the tension between the everyday and the transcendent—our struggle to grasp what lies beyond our reach. Whether hawking body parts in a Midwestern city, orbiting through the galleries of a Paris museum or plotting sibling tortures in an Arizona desert, his characters lead us through a series of dilemmas of universal appeal. "Stories…that imbue the ordinary with the extraordinary" —Siri Hustvedt. ISBN: 978-1480172777